THE PRACTICE CO

Devotions and reflections for whole-hearted living by Pocket Fuel.

ABOUT US

Hi, I'm Liz. I hope these devotions can be for you what they've been for us. From having everything figured out, to feeling the world shift beneath our feet, what's kept us moving forward is a spiritual practice. When we started Pocket Fuel six years ago, the practice of writing daily got me through some tough times. The practice of exploring the scriptures got me brave and curious and questioning. The practice of giving words to others continues to bring me so much joy, I'm so grateful for this beautiful space we've created together.

Life is something we practice on the way, in the moment. We have just one wild and precious life, as Mary Oliver said; to live intentionally helps us draw out the fullness of it. So dear friend, let's practice... whether it be love, grief, hope, conflict, joy, resilience, forgiveness... whatever the season calls for. As we continue to practice, we'll continue to move forward. Whatever your spiritual practice is, I hope this book is a good companion to you and to it. All our love, Liz and Jesse.

HOW TO READ

The Practice Co is a series of devotionals and reflections centred around this one thing: the integration of the human and the holy; the ordinary and the divine. We've created the journey to be a visual and contemplative one designed to stir the senses and imagination. You can binge these devotionals like a good Netflix series, or you can take your time with them. Each piece is bite sized to give you the space to do with it what you will. Scribble in the margins, tear out pictures, spill a bit of coffee on it here and there, or leave it squeaky clean. It's our hope that you experience each page, not just read it, and that as you do, you are awakened and inspired to go deep, live fully, and revitalise a healthy sense of curiosity and faith.

OH! And if you're into sharing stuff on social media, tag us at *#thepracticeco* so that we can find you and say 'thank you.'

TABLE OF CONTENTS

2　THE PRACTICE
What is a practice?

16　THE OTHER SIDE
Are you willing to cross to the other side of your darkness and pain?

34　SACRIFICE AND SONS
What do your *really* need to sacrifice?

52　HERE I AM
Showing up to your life.

66　BEYOND THE LABEL
Make your whole life a prayer.

80　WHAT'S NEXT
How do you move forward?

94　YOUR GOOD, GOOD HEART
Keep a soft heart in a hard world.

110　RUTH
How do you know when to stay, or when to go?

> "AN OUNCE OF PRACTICE IS WORTH MORE THAN TONS OF PREACHING."
>
> *Gandhi*

"Practice is something you do as well as something you believe. Just as much as it is something you know, it's also something you learn."

PRACTICE - PART 1
Faith is a Practice

These devotionals are more a way for us to have a daily spiritual practice, than a piece of writing offering any clear spiritual advice. It's a practice to write them, read them, and engage them in our living (if that is indeed what should be done with them).

Words are just words unless they inaugurate or encourage some kind of actual practice. Faith without works is dead (James 2), but faith that empties into actions? Into lives and vocations and decisions and engagement? Words that build our worlds? (a Heschel reference for those that know...) That's stuff you can work with.

Henry Ward Beecher once said:

"There is no such thing as preaching patience into people, unless the sermon is so long that they have to practice it while they hear." (1.)

It's believed that Gandhi said:

"An ounce of practice is worth more than tons of preaching."

I would go so far to say that any daily prayer/devotional/meditative/spiritual practice that doesn't impact the WAY you LIVE is somewhat a waste of time. You need both the abstract and the practical.

You can make as many resolutions and goals and plans as you like; you can Instagram them, or beautifully letter them into that journal you bought from an expensive stationery store; you can share them with your friends and talk about them with your mum...

But unless you put resolutions and goals and plans into practice, they'll stay exactly where they are right now: in thin air.

The same goes for our ideas on Spirituality and Christianity and Faith. We say a lot of big words, and throw around a lot of big ideas, but unless those words and ideas can be broken down into our lives, they don't really make any kind of lasting difference in the world.

Faith is a practice, not a standard, or a resolution, or a goal. It's something you live into and with. It's something you get to actually practice; as in, give it a go, try again, work it out. It's something you do as well as something you believe. Just as much as it is something you know, it's also something you learn.

Practice, friends. Not because practice makes perfect, but because practice makes progress. Practice makes an idea/goal/plan a real and tangible part of our lives.

THE PRACTICE - PART 2
The Bible Isn't a Rule Book

A lot of people ask us how they can fit more Bible reading and prayer time into their busy lives. I tell them that you can read and pray all you like, but it's how those things spill into your life that really matters. The power is in the practice.

When I was a teenager, I had a checklist of dates on my wall above my bed, and every day, after I prayed for 10 minutes, and read five chapters of the Bible (if my memory serves me correctly), I would tick the box and pat myself on the back. "Well done good and faithful servant."

Nowadays, that practice seems so mute to me, so one-sided.

How do I engage the Biblical text and prayer in such a way that it becomes more than a tick in a box and a pat on the back?

Confession: I stopped reading the Bible for a few years. I just couldn't do it anymore. So much of it made sense only on paper and not in real life. Forgiveness? Compassion? Grace? Love my neighbour? And my enemy? How the heck?! And then what about all the genocide and violence and misogyny and Paul? What am I meant to do with Paul? Some parts of it made me feel good and comforted, other parts, uncomfortable and (to be honest) sick. I didn't know how to engage this book in all of its complexities. I was only ever taught how to practice reading it, not the actual practice of engaging it.

And I've discovered that there is a huge difference.

Peter Enns wrote:

"The Bible isn't a cookbook — deviate from the recipe and the soufflé falls flat... When we open the Bible and read it, we are eavesdropping on an ancient spiritual journey. That journey was recorded over a thousand-year span of time, by different writers, with different personalities, at different times, under different circumstances, and for different reasons. In the Bible, we read of encounters with God by ancient peoples, in their times and places, asking their questions, and expressed in language and ideas familiar to them. Those encounters with God were, I believe, genuine, authentic, and real. But they were also ancient — and that explains why the Bible behaves the way it does. This kind of Bible — the Bible we have — just doesn't work well as a point-by-point exhaustive and timelessly binding list of instructions about God and the life of faith. But it does work as a model for our own spiritual journey... This Bible, which preserves ancient journeys of faith, models for us our own journeys. We recognize something of ourselves in the struggles, joys, triumphs, confusions, and despairs expressed by the biblical writers. Rather than a rulebook — and we seriously have to switch metaphors here — the Bible is more a land we get to know by hiking through it and exploring its many paths and terrains." (2.)

Make your Biblical practice one of hiking and exploring. Don't expect a point by point list of do's and don't's and secrets to life. Look for the lessons in the stories.

These days my practice is less "five chapters and tick a box," and more forgetting the chapters and verses and reading the stories as they are, researching the context and the culture through books, podcasts, and articles. It includes embracing the frustration I feel when I read something I can't reconcile (like God commanding the murders of the elderly, disabled, women, and children); letting the tears fall when I recognise my own brokenness in the psalms, my anger in the prophets, and my desperation in Jesus: "My God, my God, why have you forsaken me?" (Matt 27:46.) I let the narrative guide me, make me think, bring up questions, ask those questions, and live into faith.

The Bible isn't a rulebook, but an invitation to wrestle out our faith in real time with a multitude of "witnesses" sharing their ancient journeys with us.

≈

THE PRACTICE - PART 3
There is More to Prayer

In Luke 11, Jesus' disciples asked: *"Would you teach us a model prayer that we can pray, just like John did for his disciples?" (Luke 11:1 TPT.)*

Which, when you think about it, is super interesting. These guys wanted to know how to get it right.

In the Ancient Hebrew world, a Rabbi and his disciples had their own prayer. It was part of their identity, and the prayer belonged to the group. That's why the disciples asked Jesus if he could teach them a prayer, "just like John did for his disciples." But of course, he didn't respond by teaching them the structure of a prayer; he didn't give them a set of words to recite… he invited them into a deeper connection with God, the world, and themselves.

"Whenever you pray, be sincere and not like the pretenders who love the attention they receive while praying before others in the meetings and on street corners [Jesus replied]. Believe me, they've already received in full their reward. But whenever you pray, go into your innermost chamber and be alone with Father God, praying to him in secret. And your Father, who sees all you do, will reward you openly. When you pray, there is no need to repeat empty phrases, praying like those who don't know God, for they expect God to hear them because of their many words. There is no need to imitate them, since your Father already knows what you need before you ask him." (Matt 6:5-8 TPT.)

There is more to prayer than our public words; there is more to prayer than our words being witnessed and heard and applauded. There is more to prayer than words. Since most people in Jesus' day had houses with only one or two rooms, it was an interesting suggestion to "go into your innermost chamber and pray in secret."

Perhaps it was an invitation for the disciples to embrace emptiness and solitude, to go into their hearts and interiors - their innermost chamber. Instead of filling up space with noise, get quiet and alone; enter into Presence. Allow the presence of God to fill their inner selves, not just the space around them. It's one thing to talk; it's another to listen, and it's another thing again to simply 'BE' in the presence of God. A place where words seem inadequate.

"Western culture has tended to be an extroverted culture and a "can-do" culture." Said Richard Rohr. *"Prayer too easily became an attempt to change God and aggrandise ourselves instead of what it was meant to be – an interior practice to change the one who is praying, which will always happen if we stand calmly before this uncanny and utterly safe Presence, allowing the Divine Gaze to invade and heal our unconscious, the place where 95 percent of our motivations and reactions come from. All we can really do is return the gaze."* (3.)

What is prayer but connection to the Divine? And in turn, connection with what God is connected to? How can we be present TO and WITH the Divine, and TO and WITH those we love, interact with, and share this beautiful, crazy world with? How can our prayer practice become more than just words we recite and a bed we kneel next to? To pray is to be awake, aware, and alive to Divine presence in us, around us, and among us.

THE PRACTICE - PART 4

Certain Hope

Most days, I take ten minutes to sit or lie down, and I practice breathing: in through my nose, deep into my belly, hold it for a couple of seconds, and then exhale it out through my mouth. It's a meditative practice, and it has profoundly changed my life.

We need to take about 12 to 20 breaths per minute to get enough energy and oxygen through our bodies. But most of us breathe up to 30 times a minute (43,000 breaths a day on average!). Puffed, rushed, stressed, anxious, worried, afraid, pre-occupied, on the move, going… we're too busy to stop and take a deep and nourishing breath.

We should be able to get 90% of the energy our bodies need from deep breathing, but most of us breathe too shallowly, expelling much of its goodness before it's had time to work its divine wonders into our oxygen-starved bodies.

We talk fast, eat fast, work fast, play fast, sleep fast… too fast.

When we breathe deeply, oxygen has time to circulate throughout our whole bodies, bringing goodness in and taking with it, on the exhale, the waste. But we miss out on the goodness of that breath in our bodies in more ways than one when we breathe too quick and shallow.

Hebrews 6:19 says, *"We have this certain hope like a strong, unbreakable anchor holding our souls to God himself"* (TPT.)

The word 'soul' in this passage means "breath, the essence of life."

The Ancients called God, 'Lord.' When we write the name in English, we write 'L-O-R-D.' But in ancient Hebrew, they wrote 'Y-H-V-H.' In many ancient traditions, people wouldn't say the name of God out loud: it was/is too sacred and holy to voice. 'YHVH' means the source of being and the essence of being itself.

Breath.

The Genesis story tells us that Adam laid lifeless, a pile of dust and blood and bone until YHVH breathed essence into him; filled his blood with oxygen, expanded his lungs, fired up his brain, and shook his heart into its first beat. Adam became the carrier of the breath of God – the essence of the eternal. We are dust buckets filled with the Divine: "fragile clay jars containing this great treasure." (2 Cor 4:7.)

You pronounce the letters of Y-H-V-H singularly (Hod-Hey-Vav-Hey), they are all vowels, so when you say them traditionally, it sounds like breathing in and out. The essence of 'YHVH' fills us all, from the day we take our first breath (Hod-Hey-Vav-Hey) until the day we spend our last (Hod-Hey-Vav-Hey).

John said that in the beginning, Jesus was there. Just as God's breath filled Adam, God's spirit ignites our bodies and gives us life. God has always been here, drawing us to Gods-self, permeating the world with Divine breath, connecting us all to each other.

Not by might, nor by power… but by Spirit.

YHVH (Hod-Hey-Vav-Hey).

It's just like God to take something so familiar and normal and make it holy, powerful, and the connective fabric between us all.

My daily practice is this: I breathe deeply, and as I do, I imagine that I'm not just breathing for the sake of my body, but for my spirit, too. I breathe in the essence of life. It circulates through my blood, bringing wholeness and energy, and as it finishes its course, it skims up what muck it can and leaves my body through a mighty and deliberate exhale.

It's not magic; it's not a quick fix. It's a practice. A daily discipline. Christ in me, this dust bucket, this fragile jar of clay – the hope of Glory.

Breathe God in
(Hod-Hey-Vav-Hey)

And out
(Hod-Hey-Vav-Hey).

Make it a practice.
It might just change your life.

"The way you breathe is the way you live."
— Ancient Proverb

"Forgiveness is a work, a grace, a miracle that happens on the way. It's a practice that we.... well, practice."

THE PRACTICE - PART 5
The Practice of Forgiveness

Forgiveness is not so much something we do, but a spiritual practice we embrace. It's an awkward, challenging, difficult practice, but one that brings healing like nothing else can.

What about justice?
How do I know when I've forgiven?
But I'm still angry?
Does it mean that the person/organisation/institution gets off scot-free?
What about what's owed me?
What about my damage?

Yes, forgiveness can be complicated.

If you've ever been deeply wronged and abused, used and neglected, you know that forgiveness isn't the easy gift that's talked about on Sunday mornings in our sanitised, shiny churches. It's hard, painful, and often initially (and then some) a bitter pill to swallow.

After Jesus had died and then resurrected, he met with his disciples in a house. John wrote that he breathed on them and said: "If you forgive someone's sins, they're gone for good. If you don't forgive sins, what are you going to do with them?" (John 20:23 MSG.)

In Ancient Hebrew, the word for Spirit and breath are the same: ruach. It means "air in motion." They believed that the spirit of God and the breath you're taking are one and the same: life force, energy, essence, spirit, breath.

When Jesus spoke to his disciples together collectively for the first time after his resurrection, and breathed into them – and yes, that's what the text says he did – he could have spoken about anything: judgement, kindness, hope, mercy, faith, doctrine, truth...

But he talked about forgiveness.

If the Saviour of the world, the Divine in human form, took three days to rise, then I think us mere mortals need to give ourselves time for the rising, too.

Forgiveness is a work, a grace, a miracle that happens on the way. It's a practice that we... well, practice.

It doesn't excuse or exclude our pain; it includes it. It holds your pain and honours it, then works to let it go. That's the practice. And the marks left behind? Jesus still had his scars when he rose. He showed them to Thomas that day in the house, who perhaps was not so much doubting as he was grieving; as he was unwilling to forgive the Saviour who went AWOL, and the people who killed him.

Jesus kept his scars, the truth of what happened to him, the truth of how he healed; his testimony and physical witness of forgiveness.

Resurrection is not so much death conquered as it is death forgiven.

Forgiveness is both completely exciting and utterly

terrifying. Exciting and hopeful because I want it. Terrifying and hard and even a little offensive because it means I need to practice it.

And sure. I can do that for small sins and trespasses and hurts. But those who have genuinely hurt me? Those hurting others in our world? The unseen and untold tragedies and abuses? The wars and damage and violence? The manipulation and greed? How do you forgive that?

It's in the breath. It's in Jesus showing us what kind of miracles can take place when the air in motion – our living and breathing and practice – is laced with forgiveness.

"Forgiving and being reconciled to our enemies or our loved ones are not about pretending that things are other than they are." Wrote Bishop Desmond Tutu. *"It is not about patting one another on the back and turning a blind eye to the wrong. True reconciliation exposes the awfulness, the abuse, the hurt, the truth. It could even sometimes make things worse. It is a risky undertaking but in the end it is worthwhile, because in the end only an honest confrontation with reality can bring real healing." (4.)*

THE PRACTICE - PART 6
Practice is not Perfection

Practice doesn't make perfect. At least it hasn't for me. Not with piano lessons, maths, and well, life. I keep practicing, and I'm still not perfect.

But perfection never has been, never will be, the goal.

Van Gogh wrote in a letter:

"I am always doing what I cannot do yet in order to learn how to do it." (5.)

So when it comes to prayer, Biblical knowledge, spirituality, love, hope, forgiveness, peace, faith, family, life... all of it: do what you cannot do yet in order to learn how to do it.

Here's to the learning.

Here's to the practice.

Many are quick to talk about their values but struggle to practice them. It takes courage and integrity to live what we speak (and to speak what we live), and to do so with the flux and flow that an unpredictable, uncontrollable life needs from us (breathe your way through it). And that's the thing when you practice faith rather than just claiming to have it and know it: it bends and flows and grows with you. It's a grace.

Life is something we practice. As in, it's something we do. We can live with intentionality, with an awareness and a commitment to the practice of things like compassion and grace and faith, or not.

The choice, and the practice, is as always, up to you.

≈

"ONLY WHEN WE ARE BRAVE ENOUGH TO EXPLORE THE DARKNESS WILL WE DISCOVER THE INFINITE POWER OF OUR LIGHT."

Brené Brown

"It is in the shelter of each other that the people live."
(Irish Proverb)

THE OTHER SIDE - PART 1
Walking into the Light

"Let's go across to the other side," Jesus said to his disciples. (Mark 4:35 MSG.)

They had been teaching all day, breaking bread, telling stories, listening to stories, being with people. It was late and dark, the time when they should have retired to bed in a comfortable house offered by generous hosts. But no. Jesus wanted to go to the other side of the lake.

What was on the other side?

Could they see it from the shore as Jesus told the parables of the farmer and the seed and the lamp-stand? Were they thankful that they were on this side, and not that side? Did they wonder about it all? Or was it out of sight, out of mind?

Jesus was often going to the other side - the other side of town, the other side of the well, the other side of propriety and what was expected of him. He was continually pushing boundaries and redefining inclusion.

When he said to the Disciples, "let's go to the other side," he wasn't just being geographical.

On the other side of the lake was the region of the Gerasenes. They weren't Jewish tribes, but Rome had still plowed through their towns and cities wreaking havoc on all. Judeans never crossed the lake to go to the Gerasenes. It wasn't culturally acceptable. The region was considered dark, demonic, and destructive. They stayed away.

And yet, "let's go to the other side."

So they did. The disciples packed themselves and their crazy Rabbi up into a boat and set off. You've probably heard a lot about what happened next: Jesus fell asleep, a violent and fierce storm crashed down upon them, they woke Jesus afraid for their lives, who then stood at the front of the boat and calmed the wind and waves with only his spoken word.

Mark 4:41 (NIV) tells us that:

"They were terrified and asked each other, "Who is this? Even the wind and the waves obey him!"

Who is this man who goes to the other side, and sleeps through storms, and calms the death-call of the ocean by a simple statement of "Shalom" (peace)?

To get to the other side of the lake was an effort of the mind, heart, and body. Some might even claim that the visitation of the storm was a sign they were doing the wrong thing. But whenever you cross over into unknown territory, there are battles to face, noise to calm, fear to set aside, courage to step into, faith to keep journeying on. I suggest that those battles had more to do with their hearts and minds, than the water and the waves.

When they landed on the shores of the Gerasenes, they were met by a naked man gone mad, covered in self-inflicted wounds, screeching incoherently, with broken wrist and foot chains hanging from his emaciated body. The boat had not taken them to the docks in town, but to the local cemetery. In an area considered to be demonic and oppressive, they arrived at its darkest place.

They were about to face a different kind of storm... one of going to the other side of their prejudices and fears and assumptions and preconceived ideas of health and vitality.

They were about to meet someone within whom raged a storm. What had just happened geographically in the physical world, was about to take place inwardly, in the personal, intimate rooms of a human heart. But what was to come would end up revealing another storm again that raged in the community that didn't know how to love divergence. There's an old Irish proverb that sums up this story:

"It is in the shelter of each other that the people live."

This is a story about humans and demons and affliction, but more than that, it's a story about what happens when we dare to cross to the other side of our proverbial lakes to villages and cemeteries we once thought were off limits. Are we willing to journey to the other side through whatever storm necessary to meet someone in their darkness, only to be shown our own, and walk together into the light?

THE OTHER SIDE - PART 2
Closing the Divide

"They arrived on the other side of the sea in the country of the Gerasenes. As Jesus got out of the boat, a madman from the cemetery came up to him. He lived there among the tombs and graves. No one could restrain him—he couldn't be chained, couldn't be tied down. He had been tied up many times with chains and ropes, but he broke the chains, snapped the ropes. No one was strong enough to tame him. Night and day he roamed through the graves and the hills, screaming out and slashing himself with sharp stones." Mark 5:1-5 (MSG).

Some of us take all the talk of demons with a grain of salt. Surely these were ancient, primitive cultures, who didn't know what we know about mental illness, or science, and so branded every seemingly adverse reaction as the work of demonic forces. On the other side of that, some of us believe in demons like we believe in God. Satan is real, as are his minions, who inflict the earth with evil and pain, who work in the shadows slowly controlling humanity by its propensity for sin and destruction.

I grew up in a vibrant Pentecostal Church. We really liked casting out demons. We prayed and shouted at Satan "In Jesus Name" and were preached at about the dangers of demonic possession. I've witnessed a few exorcisms, and my skin still prickles at their memory.

And this man of the Gerasenes? He was often our object lesson.

But he was not an object (revelation). He was a flesh and blood human being with complex issues in a society that didn't know how to love him.

Fyodor Dostoyevsky said:

"Nothing is easier than to denounce the evildoer; nothing is more difficult than to understand him."

I discovered that I've been (am) a flesh and blood human dealing with complex issues in an organisation that didn't know how to love me. I've discovered it by observing and knowing other flesh and blood humans dealing with complex issues in a society, country, and nation that doesn't know how to love them either...

I've seen enough from humans to be skeptical of demon possession. We are entirely capable of inflicting evil upon each other without any help from anyone else. I've experienced enough spiritually to be suspicious of the absence of an evil entity at work in the world. I'm equally concerned about people who blame Satan for things that go wrong in life, and those who pay no attention or give no credence to the spiritual.

Some people would rather blame the Devil for their plight (and that of others) than take responsibility for it (and them). It's much easier to scream at an invisible force than it is to face yourself.

I know some people, including me, who feel caught in an otherworldly net of habit and shame and fear. Controlled by a presence outside of our own.

René Girard said:

"The devil's "quintessential being," the source from which he draws his lies, is the violent contagion that has no substance to it. The devil does not have a stable foundation; he has no being at all. To clothe himself in the semblance of being, he must act as a

parasite on God's creatures." (1.)

Evil manifests most powerfully in how we treat ourselves and each other. It grows in power and strength every time we choose to participate in division.

The Gerasene man was a soul beyond himself, experiencing some kind of life controlling force within his body. But if we look carefully, we'll discover that he's more like us than we care to admit. Demons and all.

And it would seem that Jesus was most careful to understand him, not denounce him.

After all, he came from the other side to get close to him… bridging the divide.

THE OTHER SIDE - PART 3

Overcome Evil with Good

Many stories in the Bible involving demons and possession are about illnesses (mental or physical), unexpected weather patterns, war and occupation; things going really wrong. In the Ancient Near East, where they didn't have modern technology, devices, machines, techniques, and knowledge to handle and interpret the disasters they faced, it was logical to blame an evil power. Just as it was logical to ascribe all goodness that happened to God. Good things: Thanks, God! Bad things: curse the devil, cast him out.

Moreover, none of the languages of the ancient Near East, including Hebrew, have a word that translates to "demon" in English. Back then, a demon was a being less powerful than God and less endowed with individuality and personality. Where God was accorded regular public worship, demons were not; they were dealt with in magic rites in individual cases of human suffering, which is their particular sphere of work.

It's not as simple as saying, "the Bible says it, that settles it." There's culture, nuance and context to take into consideration, too.

When we talk about evil, we're talking about that which is categorically opposed and resistant to goodness. I've heard too many stories to deny the presence of beings devoid of physical bodies. I've been in situations where what the person was wrestling with went way beyond their own mind and body. I have seen things that have forced me to create a category for the disembodied but real. Language in our scriptures, and others, are our attempts at different times and seasons and cultures to grasp the physical reality of the seemingly metaphysical one.

Back to the Gerasenes man: Mark 5 goes on to say:

"What business do you have, Jesus, Son of the High God, messing with me? I swear to God, don't give me a hard time!" (Jesus had just commanded the tormenting evil spirit, "Out! Get out of the man!")

Jesus asked him, "Tell me your name."

He replied, "My name is Legion. I'm a rioting mob." Then he desperately begged Jesus not to banish them from the country." (Mark 5:6-10 MSG.)

There are a few interesting points here that we'll cover in part 4, but suffice to say that the man who met Jesus and his disciples that day stark naked in the cemetery, was a man beyond himself.

Richard Rohr said:

"Most people I know are overly identified with their own thoughts and feelings. They don't really have feelings; their feelings have them. That may be what earlier Christians meant by being "possessed" by a demon. That's why so many of Jesus' miracles are the exorcism of devils. Most don't take that literally anymore, but the devil is still a powerful metaphor, which demands that you take it quite seriously. Everyone has a few devils. I know I'm "possessed" at least once or twice a day, even if just for a few minutes! There are all kinds of demons—in other words, there are lots of times when you cannot not think a certain way." (2.)

Rohr goes on to talk about the many times Jesus cast demons out of people in the New Testament and draws a parallel to what we know to be the disease of addiction. Demon possession could have been our ancestor's way of naming the disease. It does behave like a possession to the person ensnared in its grip. And it's often only expelled when we name it in front of witnesses, or listen to those who love us name it for us.

Whatever demon possession is, and whatever our friend the Gerasene was experiencing, I don't think it's an either/or... is it real or not. I believe it's a YES, AND: a collection of all these things and more. The danger is that we don't take evil seriously, and the danger is that we take it too seriously.

Whatever you believe about the origin and power of evil, Paul made this suggestion in Romans 12:21 (NIV):

"Do not be overcome by evil, but overcome evil with good."

Overcome it by showering it with more and more and more of what it exists to resist until you overwhelm it.

THE OTHER SIDE - PART 4
Legion

There are two sides to every story. Sometimes (most of the time), even more. After spending the day telling parables and hanging out with people on the beach, Jesus packed up his mates and went to the other side of the lake. Which was no small thing.

There on the other side, they met a man beyond himself: screaming incoherently and covered in wounds and broken chains and dirt and hair and God knows what else. When Jesus tried to cast demons out of him, Mark says that they refused to go. So he asked them their name. And they replied:

"My name is Legion. I'm a rioting mob." Then he desperately begged Jesus not to banish them from the country. A large herd of pigs was browsing and rooting on a nearby hill. The demons begged him, "Send us to the pigs so we can live in them." Jesus gave the order. But it was even worse for the pigs than for the man. Crazed, they stampeded over a cliff into the sea and drowned." (Mark 5:10-13 MSG.)

The Gerasenes had been invaded by the Roman empire, too. Just like their Jewish neighbours, the Romans took nearly all they had and left nothing but devastation in their wake.

A 'legion' was what a Roman fighting unit was called, and it was made up of typically six thousand soldiers (my name is Legion...). "Interestingly the Roman 10th legion, the Legio X Fretensis, was based in Syro-Palestine [Gerasenes] and had a wild boar as the insignia on its standards and seal." (3.)

The political message in the imagery of this story cannot and should not be avoided. Any political move by any government at any time that oppresses people, and uses them as collateral damage in games of domination and wealth and winning and outsmarting, is "demonic."

Make no mistake. The Romans ruled with violence and fear and torture. Who knows what this man had witnessed in his town, in his own home, to his own person? The legions, at their wildest and most irresponsible, were guilty of atrocities that would make the blood run cold. Trauma twists people up inside. Drives them mad with grief and pain and rage. "PTSD is a whole-body tragedy, an integral human event of enormous proportions with massive repercussions," said Susan Pease Banitt (4). The word Legion conjured a vision of terror and death and destruction. He was convinced that demons not unlike the Roman army that devastated his village were inside him.

And how do you recover from trauma so devastating? You name it. With others.

For people who have been through horrific circumstances, and battled the insane tightrope of shame and heartache as a result, being validated and naming the source of pain is the beginning of freedom.

So, were there actual demons? Was this a political message that Mark recorded (note that Mark's book was written at least thirty years after these events took place...)? I think, yes and yes. Both. In ways we would do well to be humbled by.

Frederick Buechner said:

"God knows we have our own demons to be cast out, our own uncleanness to be cleansed. Neurotic anxiety happens to be my own particular demon, a floating sense of doom that has ruined many of what could have been, should have been, the happiest days of my life, and more than a few times in my life I have been raised from such ruins, which is another way of saying that more than a few times in my life I have been raised from death - death of the spirit anyway, death of the heart - by the healing power that Jesus calls us both to heal with and to be healed by." (5.)

THE OTHER SIDE - PART 5
Collateral Damage

Jesus ventured across the lake, through a storm, into a cemetery, to find a man in need of help. The details in Mark 5 describe this man as being possessed by thousands of demons and driven to the edge of sanity. The story has some disturbing elements if we dare to pay attention.

"As Jesus got out of the boat, a madman from the cemetery came up to him. He lived there among the tombs and graves." (Mark 5:2-3 MSG.)

Had he always lived there? Or was he sent there? Banished? Outcast? Was no one caring for him?

"No one could restrain him..." (Mark 5:3 MSG.)

Someone tried to restrain him? Why? Was it because he was a danger to others? To himself? Were they afraid of what they couldn't explain or refused to understand? Was the community ashamed of him, and tried to keep him "tied down," out of the way. Did they chain him up and leave him?

"He couldn't be chained, couldn't be tied down. He had been tied up many times with chains and ropes, but he broke the chains, snapped the ropes. No one was strong enough to tame him. Night and day he roamed through the graves and the hills, screaming out and slashing himself with sharp stones." (Mark 5:4-5 MSG.)

Was he screaming and lashing out because he had been chained and restrained? Or was he chained because he was screaming and lashing out? The man's presence in the cemetery becomes a question of society: Where was everyone? And was it that all they did to heal him was to tie him up in fetters and chains?

Before you say, "Liz, you're reaching here," take a moment to think about how we treat our wounded. How we treat ourselves when we're wounded. How, in our communities, we create the demons within people, and then shame them for having them. How often do we send our wounded and compromised to the proverbial graveyard to die alone? How is that someone's lament and protest and pain becomes the means by which we persecute them? Here's what happened after Jesus cast out the man's demons:

"Those tending the pigs, scared to death, bolted and told their story in town and country. Everyone wanted to see what had happened. They came up to Jesus and saw the madman sitting there wearing decent clothes and making sense, no longer a walking madhouse of a man. Those who had seen it told the others what had happened to the demon-possessed man and the pigs. At first they were in awe—and then they were upset, upset over the drowned pigs. They demanded that Jesus leave and not come back." (Mark 5:14-17 MSG.)

This community was more concerned about economics than the health of one of its members. And if that's how they treated one man, you can bet that others fell victim to the same conduct. They saw a man once possessed by thousands of demons set free. And they were afraid... Perhaps they were afraid of Jesus's power... he had apparently sent the demons into the pigs, and they all died. That's pretty freaky. But more than that, maybe they were afraid that they had been found out. Their intentions had been unveiled, witnessed. Discovered. Just like my kids when they're in trouble, and they demand that I not look at them and go away and leave them alone because they can't bear the shame of being seen in the light of their wrongdoings, perhaps these villagers couldn't bear to see the man they had written off healed and whole, and they couldn't bear their shame to be as naked as he once was.

We belittle those who are in trouble, those who are so close to the edge of life and trauma. We put economics and progress above individuals creating a culture that accepts collateral damage as the norm. All the while, we fail to realise that it is by lifting others up that healing comes. Not just to them, but to us all.

"Be here, now... in all of this, because even here, in this mess and heartache and misunderstanding are the seeds of hope and wonder."

THE OTHER SIDE - PART 6
The Seeds of Hope and Wonder

Eight times in the book of Mark, people begged Jesus for things:

A leper for healing.
The demons for the pigs.
Jairus for his daughter.
The sick for Jesus's clothes.
A woman for her daughter.
A blind man for sight.
Bartimaeus for mercy.

These seven received what they asked. The one time Jesus denied someone's plea was for our friend the Gerasene:

"As Jesus was getting into the boat, the demon-delivered man begged to go along, but he wouldn't let him." (Mark 5:18 MSG.)

You would think that Jesus would have wholeheartedly consented! You would think that it was a reasonable request! That after everything this man had endured, Jesus would have compassionately granted his plea.

Nope.

Sometimes, we want to be taken away. We want to escape what's going on, what has gone on, start new, somewhere different with different people and different circumstances. But we have to face our demons. We have to be where we are.

Jesus said to him: *"Go home to your own people." (Mark 5:19 MSG.)*

The town probably would have preferred he left with Jesus, too. Then all talk and responsibility for what had gone down between them could have been swept under the rug and forgotten. But it doesn't matter whether we stay or whether we go; if we don't face our demons, they remain with us, gathering strength, waiting to strike.

When we face ourselves - our demons and our challenges and whatever is happening here and now within us and around us - there is the possibility that you can turn a terrible narrative around. The place we think no life can come from is often the birthplace of generosity and goodness. And when we face our demons? When we submit ourselves to the work of transformation? We realise that our demons aren't so scary. They're not demons at all, but our teachers willing to serve us if we submit ourselves to the work of owning our own lives. Then, the hostility in our bodies can become a place of hospitality.

Mark went on to say: *"So the man left and went into the region of Jordan and parts of Syria to tell everyone he met about what Jesus had done for him, and all the people marvelled!" (Mark 5:20 MSG.)*

And really, the exorcism that took place is less about devils and more about fear and hostility and assumption and division. Not just for the man gone mad living in the cemetery, but for his friends, and family, and town, too. We rarely sit with the end of this story and consider what it meant for the man to return home. I think it's a picture of what it means to courageously live within your own story. Jesus told him that he needed to be where he was. 'Be here, now...' in all of this, because even here, in this mess and heartache and misunderstanding are the seeds of hope and wonder.

Brené Brown said:

"Owning our story can be hard but not nearly as difficult as spending our lives running from it. Embracing our vulnerabilities is risky but not nearly as dangerous as giving up on love and belonging and joy—the experiences that make us the most vulnerable. Only when we are brave enough to explore the darkness will

we discover the infinite power of our light."
(6.)

We don't have to leave to escape. Substances, TV, food, shopping, social media, apps (but not ours *wink*), pornography, even things like cleaning and exercise and remembering the past and dreaming about the future, are all escape portals that take us away from here. Owning our story is about taking responsibility, doing the work, accepting the challenge, drinking in all that life is and has to offer which at any moment could be lessons, healing, redemption, rest, joy, grief, sadness, suffering, compassion, mercy... all equally capable of bringing different shades of beauty and grace into our lives we would have missed had we escaped into the things we do. Being here now is about showing up to your life in all your messy, beautiful, glory.

Sometimes, not getting what we think is essential for our survival is exactly what we need.

"Go home to your own people." No running, no hiding.

Face it all.

And find the light.

THE OTHER SIDE - PART 7
Willing to Cross

"The Gospel of Mark carries the theme: How do we move through suffering" -Dr Alexander Shaia (1).

The story in Mark 5 about a man driven mad, living in a cemetery, filled with all kinds of demons, is a story about how suffering cripples both its host and the ones around it when we don't embrace it healthily and wholeheartedly.

And yes, suffering is to be embraced. Our pain and tragedies are not something to hide in unmarked graves and dark corners, chained and tied up, so they stay where we've put them, well behaved and silent. The more we try to repress our suffering the louder it howls and the more violent it becomes.

It's also a story about going to the other side of suffering until you land on the shores of healing.

The village had tried to cure the man by restraining him and tried to cure the problem he created in the town, by banishing him. Cure and healing are two different things.

Many of us want the quick fix, one tablet, single procedure, in and out, give me the script, do it for me now, remedy. We want the demons to be driven out. We want to escape to new lands and clean slates. We want to run from suffering and responsibility. We want to be cured.

But healing is another thing entirely. Healing requires you to face your demons (which are less demons and more your own personal pain - which is far from demonic. We need to end the culture of demonising mental illness and any kind of suffering). Healing requires that we return home instead of escaping. To do the work, to be vulnerable and courageous. Healing is what happens when you move through suffering with awareness, company, and love. It's not a quick fix, but it is a game changer. A life changer. And instead of a clean slate, you get redemption.

"Let's go to the other side," said Jesus. (Mark 4:35 MSG.)

Let's move all the way through our fears, demons (proverbial or otherwise), prejudices, limiting beliefs, assumptions, sufferings, grief... all of it, until we get to the other side. Face your life all the way through. It's how you find healing, and it's how you bring healing to others, too.

This little story in Mark 5 that is so misunderstood and under-appreciated because of the hurried nature of our reading and our lack of curiosity, is a complicated, beautiful story about suffering. Finding those who suffer and being with them. Finding ourselves in our suffering and owning it. Witnessing our suffering to others so they can learn from it.

Helen Keller said:

"The world is full of suffering, but it is also full of the overcoming of it."

Open your eyes, be here, now, and see.

Then, it's the challenge to cross to the other side of how we treat and perceive those in our community we don't know what to do with, those who don't fit inside our carefully drawn lines for whatever reason. It's not just about treating them better, but respecting them, learning from them, dignifying them and their stories. Realising that they don't have to fit inside our carefully drawn lines. Perhaps our lines need to be erased altogether. We don't have to know what to "do with" people, we only have to know what to do for them: love.

This is a story about humans and demons and affliction, but more than that, it's a story about what happens when we dare to cross to the other side of our proverbial lakes to villages and cemeteries we once thought were off limits. Are we willing to cross over to the other side through whatever storm necessary to meet someone else in their darkness, only to be shown our own, and walk together into the light?

A PROMISE IS A CLOUD,
FULFILMENT IS RAIN.

SACRIFICE AND SONS - PART 1
The Promise

Father Abraham had many sons. Eventually.

He had eight kids, but for most of the stories told about him, Abraham had but two. And they came pretty late in life. We call him Father Abraham, the patriarch of our faith, the father of many nations, whose children are as numerous as the stars. "I am one of them and so are you. So let's all praise the Lord."

Even though God promised Abraham that his descendants would fill the earth, we forget that in his lifetime, his family unit was anything but numerous and conventional.

Back when he was called Abram, God said to him:

"Leave your country, your family, and your father's home for a land that I will show you. I'll make you a great nation and bless you. I'll make you famous; you'll be a blessing. I'll bless those who bless you; those who curse you I'll curse. All the families of the Earth will be blessed through you." (Gen 12:1-3 MSG.)

I wonder what his family thought? Did they try and make him stay? Did they disown him because of his decision? Did they tell him he could never come back?

Abram left with his wife Sarai, and his brother Lot. Together they had many adventures. Promises were made about kids and generations. His name got changed to Abraham, and Sarai to Sarah. He and his brother parted ways. Sarah, who hadn't fallen pregnant, told him to have sex with her servant (without her servant's consent) so that they could get the promise fulfilled. Hagar birthed Abram a son, and the love he had for him, Ishmael, spurred hatred and jealousy in Sarah. So, Ishmael and his mother, Hagar, were exiled. Abraham was the first person to get circumcised (that would have been an interesting conversation). He accepted foreigners and strangers into his camp/tribe. He was visited by angels, had visions, and communed with the Divine on the regular. He argued with God about the destruction of Sodom and Gomorrah and called God a hypocrite while doing so. Finally, Sarah fell pregnant to Abraham, and they had a son. They were old and weary and tested. And yet, their long-awaited promise arrived.

Isaac. An anchor to knowing that the Divine could be trusted.

That is until God asked Abraham to kill the only son that he had living with him. The son he loved more than anything in the world, through whom the visions and prophecies would be fulfilled. The son that had been promised to him by the same God who now commanded he be killed.

If I were Abraham, I would have said,

"Nope. No. Not happening."

But, seemingly, Abraham set out to obey this weird, random, violent command.

Was it a test of his faith? Was God being double-minded? Did God forget the promise God made? Did God change God's mind? What kind of God asks a person to kill his own son?

Or was something new, radical, and different happening in the life of Abraham and the world at that time?

God told Abraham that all people on earth would be blessed through him and his offspring. Perhaps God was trying to show him how.

≈

SACRIFICE AND SONS - PART 2
The Aching Question

"Leave your country, your family, and your father's home for a land that I will show you." God told Abram (Gen 12:1 MSG.)

This was new. At this point in time, life was tribal. You stuck with your tribe. You lived with your tribe. You ate with your tribe. You married within your tribe. You killed with your tribe, or you were killed with your tribe. But to leave your tribe? In a world that had no maps or dictionaries or google or knowledge about what was beyond their borders? Abram may have been the most progressive man of his day. God was doing something NEW through him. And that new thing? In a world where tribalism ruled, and you had to kill, or you were killed, Abram would start a new tribe that would BLESS. This was revolutionary.

We still live quite tribally, if you think about it, and the call to bless rather than to curse is alive and well.

As well as land and notoriety and blessing, God promised Abraham descendents. Which meant that he would have children. Which meant that Sarah would fall pregnant. Which seemed unlikely as time went by. That's the thing with newness, right? It never feels possible. At the outset, the destination seems out of reach. The promise seems absurd. Ridiculous even. But that's all that Abraham had when he left his fathers land: a promise.

Promises are problematic. We are quick to make them and slow to follow through, if we follow through at all. Always be careful when you promise in words that you follow through in action, or that you communicate well when things don't go according to the promise. Promises aren't suggestions or ideas or what ifs. A promise is a sacred commitment. When God promised Abraham that God would do something new through him; and then later, when God asked Abraham to count the stars because that's how many descendants he would have, God wasn't making a suggestion or putting forward an idea. It was a promise. New tribe. New life. Promise.

But in Genesis 22, God said to Abraham:

"Take your dear son Isaac whom you love and go to the land of Moriah. Sacrifice him there as a burnt offering on one of the mountains that I'll point out to you."

Does this request shock you? Because it should. That's why the story is in the Biblical text. It's meant to make you think, search, and ask questions. If it doesn't, then you're not reading it right. Why would God ask this? Wouldn't it be a breach of the promise? Can God go back on God's word? Is God above Gods own law or is God intrinsically connected to Divine law that God must follow what God institutes? And then there's this pervading question:

What kind of God would ask a father to murder his son? Because that question leads us somewhere else.

There's an ancient proverb that says: "A promise is a cloud, fulfilment is rain." Abraham had seen both the cloud and the rain. The promise and the fulfilment. The big question for him now was: Wwould God go back on God's word? The answer is in the drama of the story itself. It's a narrative that's going somewhere. Perhaps rather than testing Abraham, the whole story shows us that God doesn't go back on promises. Perhaps Abraham's faith wasn't in the fact that a sacrifice replacement would appear and Isaac would be saved, but that through him and this story all would understand that God would never require that kind of sacrifice.

God would never ask for the rain back.

SACRIFICE AND SONS - PART 3
Sacrifice and Splitting Hairs

Abraham's firstborn, Ishmael, came to be in horrific circumstances. Tired of her pain, Sarah told Abraham to have sex with her servant (Genesis 16), Hagar, to try and conceive a child that they would take as their own; that would become the promise. Keep in mind that Hagar had no choice in the matter. This was not a happy arrangement. And the pain continued after Hagar gave birth to Ishmael. It became clear that Ishmael would never be Sarah's. Fast forward a score of years, some crazy stories, an angel visitation to reiterate the promise of a child, and Sarah fell pregnant. Nine months later, Isaac was born.

The tension between Ishmael and Isaac - or more accurately, Sarah and Hagar - and the circumstances that led them to where they were, proved too much for everyone, so Sarah kicked Ishmael and Hagar out of the tribe. (A story for another day...)

Abraham had two sons whom he loved. One was exiled, and the other...

"Take your dear son Isaac whom you love and go to the land of Moriah. Sacrifice him there as a burnt offering on one of the mountains that I'll point out to you." (Genesis 22:2 MSG.)

Child sacrifice was a thing back in Abraham's time.

They didn't have the technology or the science yet to tell them why sometimes their crops grew or died. They didn't know why people got sick, or they didn't win a war, or why the animals died, or why things thrived. For them, it all came back to whether they had pleased the Gods or not. And how did you please the Gods? By giving to them. By making a sacrifice. And if things got super bad, you needed to give a super amazing sacrifice. And what is more super amazing than a child?

So when God asked Abraham to sacrifice his son, it's not something he had never heard of before. The tribe he left behind may have even practiced the morbid tradition. God was addressing a cultural practice that was well known in Abraham's day.

Just a couple of chapters before, God visited Abraham and told him that he wanted to destroy Sodom and Gomorrah. And Abraham:

"Stood in God's path, blocking his way and confronted him,

"Are you serious? Are you planning on getting rid of the good people right along with the bad? What if there are fifty decent people left in the city; will you lump the good with the bad and get rid of the lot? Wouldn't you spare the city for the sake of those fifty innocents? I can't believe you'd do that, kill off the good and the bad alike as if there were no difference between them. Doesn't the Judge of all the Earth judge with justice?" (Gen 19:22-25 MSG.)

He challenged the Divine. Bargained with God. Called God out, even. Begged for the lives of complete strangers.

But when asked to kill his son? After he had already lost his first son to jealousy and the desert? No arguments, no bargains, no protest. He set off at first light.

Hang on... This is about sacrifice, right? Abraham is acting on faith in the Divine. He's obedient which is honourable and holy. Or...

Something else is going on?

A telling line is this:

When Abraham, Isaac, and his servants arrived at the place of the sacrifice, *"Abraham told his two young servants, "Stay here with the donkey. The boy and I are going over there to worship; then we'll come back to you.""* (Gen 22:5 MSG.)

Did you see it? Abraham said to his servants "WE" as in he and Isaac, both of them, together, will return. He submitted himself to the narrative of the story to serve a greater purpose.

You might think I'm splitting hairs here, but what if this story isn't about being willing to sacrifice your children (your most beloved connection) to obey God and prove yourself faithful? What kind of God would toy with a person like that?

What if it's about a God who would never ask us to do that in the first place?

In a day and age where our kids (or most beloved connections) are often the sacrificial lambs to our ministries, careers, and things even more trivial that serve our cravings, this story couldn't be more timely.

SACRIFICE AND SONS - PART 4
Properly Fixed and Fit Together

The story of Abraham and Isaac has always troubled me.

I was preacher's daughter and spent most of my spare time at Church, or church events, or church-related events at my parent's house, or another pastor's house. Our whole life centred around Church. There was a lot of beauty to it, for sure. I have many happy memories of that time. But it had a deep, dark, shadow side, too.

We sacrificed everything for Church. And when we used to read this passage in Genesis 22 about Abraham's willingness to sacrifice his son, I would shudder in my seat.

At times, I often felt like Isaac walking to his death with someone he trusted. Would I be sacrificed? Would God provide a ram, a sacrifice replacement, for me? Would I be a lamb led to slaughter? Would I be asked to sacrifice others for the sake of the Kingdom? For the longest time, I believed that if I really trusted God, and if I really had faith in the Divine, I should walk willingly toward the altar, whether I'm taken there, or walk myself there. "Though he slay me, yet will I trust him" type stuff. (Job 13:15). I thought Church was more important than me; more important than my mental and physical health, academic pursuits, my sense of self, my passions... it was bigger and more valuable. The individual gives way to the community; collateral damage part of the story. And like Isaac seemed to give himself willingly, I did, too. It was what you did, right? That's what trust is, right? That's how you prove to God that you'd follow God anywhere, right?

No.

Trust is not blindly following someone. Trust is not walking toward a blood-stained altar while your companion holds the knife. Some may actually call that abuse.

The promise God gave to Abraham about descendants and blessing belonged to Isaac, too. He would have heard the stories, perhaps around the campfire at night while staring into the starry heavens wondering how many children he would have, and what things he would do to bless the earth, rather than curse it. What was going through Isaacs mind and heart that day when his father was willing to kill him because of how much he loved God?

The story doesn't add up.

All through the Old Testament, the Divine condemned child sacrifice.

God told Abraham that God was going to do something NEW, different, revolutionary, through him. Something that would bring blessing to EVERYONE. Child sacrifice was not new, and it didn't prove to bless anyone or anything.

So when God created a scene that would be told again and again and again, about a man with a promise of newness and blessing, who was asked to sacrifice that promise in line with age-old traditions, who was then saved from sacrificing that promise – rescued from repeating the same pattern of sacrifice and violence of all the other tribes – we have to ask ourselves, what's the message in the drama?

Because that's a function of ancient Hebrew literature. The drama is part of the story. The more dramatic, the bigger the point.

"Isaac spoke up and said, "Father?"
"Yes, my son?" Abraham replied.
"The fire and wood are here," Isaac said, "but where is

the lamb for the burnt offering?"

Abraham answered, "God himself will provide the lamb for the burnt offering, my son." And the two of them went on together." (Genesis 22:7-8 NIV.)

God will provide. Was Abraham submitting to God's command, or was he participating in an unfolding drama of what blessing looks like?

We are so used to the dualistic idea of 'either/or,' of 'you can't have both,' it's 'all or nothing,' that we fail to see the subtle language and nuance of this revolutionary story. I grew up believing that this story was my death sentence. God would one day ask me, perhaps always ask me, to give up what I love in order to achieve what I was born for. OR, that I would be the something given up.

I have done the former and experienced the latter, and neither was a holy occurrence.

Life is not a zero-sum game. And yes, while sacrifices happen, and they must, sometimes the bigger test of faith and trust lies in what you don't willingly offer on an altar.

SACRIFICE AND SONS - PART 5

Here I Am

In ancient Hebrew, the word for sacrifice is 'korban.' It suggests a loss or the giving up of something. Although that is certainly a part of the ritual of sacrifice, it's not at all the literal meaning of the Hebrew word. The word 'korban' comes from the word 'karev,' which means 'to draw near,' and tells us that the primary purpose of sacrifice is to draw near to the Divine.

Sacrifice isn't required to make God happy, or to pay a debt, or to turn away wrath, or to gain grace. We sacrifice some things to grow closer to other things.

The Divine is inclusive, gracious, loving. God commands us to love one another, and ourselves, as we love God. The Divine has threaded this trinitarian connective idea into scripture from the very beginning. Think Adam and Eve, Cain and Abel... and now Abraham and Isaac. We are, in a way, each other's keepers.

When God asked Abraham to sacrifice his son, it was not a new idea in that day and age that to be appeased, a God would require a great sacrifice. It happened all the time. People delivered up their first born child hoping to gain favour with the Gods, which would manifest in provision, protection, and prosperity.

Perhaps not much has changed.

Perhaps we are still caught in the cycle of offering up that which has been entrusted to us hoping that that act will gain us more personal protection, freedom, rights, and fortune. Perhaps we are quick to devalue life and even quicker to hoard our own.

Although this story is ancient, its message is as relevant as ever. We have been entrusted with each other... are we busy walking others to the altar of sacrifice? Or are we seeking freedom for those we share the planet with?

Abraham seemed willing to walk his son Isaac to the altar. It seemed that he was willing to kill his son to prove his faithfulness to God. But something else was going on. An intervention took place, which made this story different from every other child sacrifice story heard and seen at the time.

God stopped proceedings. He put an end to it. He called out to Abraham, and Abraham replied:

"Here I am."

Hineni (Hebrew for "here I am") is a word that has been saving my life. "Here I am" isn't a geographical indication, it's an offering of presence. Here I am, at this moment, witnessing this exchange, and giving it my full attention. Aware, awake, alive, to the Divine at work within me, around me, and through me. This phrase, hineni, was used at transformational moments. Abraham's use of it here tells us that something significant and life-changing was happening.

Unlike the other Gods worshipped at Abraham's time, this God, Yahweh, was a God who provided, rather than demanded; was a God who gave, rather than a God who took first-born children. Was a God of blessing, rather than a God of cursing. Relational, gracious, inclusive. A God who would sacrifice God's own deity and self (if God has a self) to come close to those Divinely beloved (everyone).

As the drama unfolded, Abraham raised his arm, ready to kill his son, when God called out and stopped him. He looked up - he stopped and looked around and saw a ram in the bushes.

If only we could be present enough - Here I am - to spot the difference between sacrifice and atrocity.

SACRIFICE AND SONS - PART 6
There is Always an Alternative

Was Abraham's faith tested when God asked him to sacrifice his son as a burnt offering? Or was God putting to the test the whole idea of child sacrifice? The notion that we have to sacrifice that which is intrinsically valuable to us in order to create intimacy with the Divine? Was the lamb caught in the thicket a reward for Abraham's blind obedient faith?

An Ancient Jewish text, The Pirkei Avot (Sayings of the Ancestors) - a section of the Mishnah (a rabbinic compilation of legal material in which they broke down the Torah and 'argue' about what it could mean) - quotes a list of crazy unexplainable things that were created on the last day of Creation. These things have no rhyme or reason or rational. God created them as exceptions to the rules of nature and history (Pirkei Avot 5:8).

And guess what's on this list?

"The ram for Abraham, our father."

Yep.

Now, look. I don't think the Rabbi's who wrote the Mishnah meant that this ram had been caught in that bush since the dawn of time for the very moment that Abraham would see it right before nearly killing his son. I believe it's included in the list of crazy miraculous things because they didn't know how else to

try to explain what was going on in the story.

What if the miracle wasn't in the providence of the ram? What if the ram wasn't Abrahams reward of faith? What if the greater miracle was in Abraham?

"Abraham looked up and there in a thicket he saw a ram caught by its horns." (Genesis 22:13 NIV.)

Perhaps Abraham was so focused on his dreadful and apparently inescapable task that he couldn't see what was there, right nearby, in plain sight. Perhaps what had been there all along.

Abraham had to turn not only his hand but his heart away from the idea that God really demanded such an awful sacrifice. Abraham was able to undergo a change of spiritual understanding just in time to see that there was an alternative way to create intimacy with God.

The relevance of this ram being on the list (in the Pirkei Avot) of crazy, miraculous, unexplainable things that were created on the last day of creation, isn't to suggest that this was a supernatural ram of sorts, but that from the very beginning, God never intended for Abraham to kill Isaac. God didn't change God's mind on a whim, or an act of faith. It was always God's plan that Isaac live. But the ability to see the ram? The fact that Abraham lifted his eyes and saw an alternative? That's the deeper, everyday kind of miracle.

We live in a world where tragic, unnecessary, and un-asked for sacrifices, are committed on the regular. Ministry, career, destructive habits, perceived standards, peer pressure, government pressure, oppression, greed, racism, misogyny, inequality… these all sacrifice the innocent on the altar of "give me more, provide for me, protect me." The problem is, the 'God' we're offering our sacrifices to – wealth, reputation, certainty, security, addiction, and more – is never satisfied. It always demands more than what we can give. More than what we can afford.

But the Divine? God provides, gives, and blesses. God is a God who wants us to forgive our enemies so that we don't keep the circulation of violence spiralling out of control. God wants us to love our neighbours. And hey, God wants us to cherish our children, physically and spiritually, not sacrifice them.

The story of Abraham and Isaac is thousands of years old. But it's a modern one, too.

The ram is always there, there is always an alternative if we are present enough to lift up our eyes and see.

SACRIFICE AND SONS - PART 7
The Gift of Sacrifice

What's important to you?
What do you spend your nights worrying about?
What do you spend your days dreaming about?
What makes you angry, happy, or sad?
What makes a bad day?
Who do you want to please?
Whose approval are you after?
Do you care when you're misunderstood? And by whom?
Do you chase the thrill? Or crave silence?
Who would you give anything to work with?

What would you give everything to have?

How much do you promise, and to whom?

What makes a gift sacrificial?

For the ancient Jews, the focus of sacrifice wasn't so much what they lost in the act, but in what they gained. In Hebrew, the word for sacrifice means 'to draw near.' What you sacrifice for is what you draw near to yourself.

Just make sure that at the end of the day you haven't sacrificed the ones you were given to sacrifice for.

"Sometimes the bigger test of faith and trust lies in what you don't willingly offer on an altar."

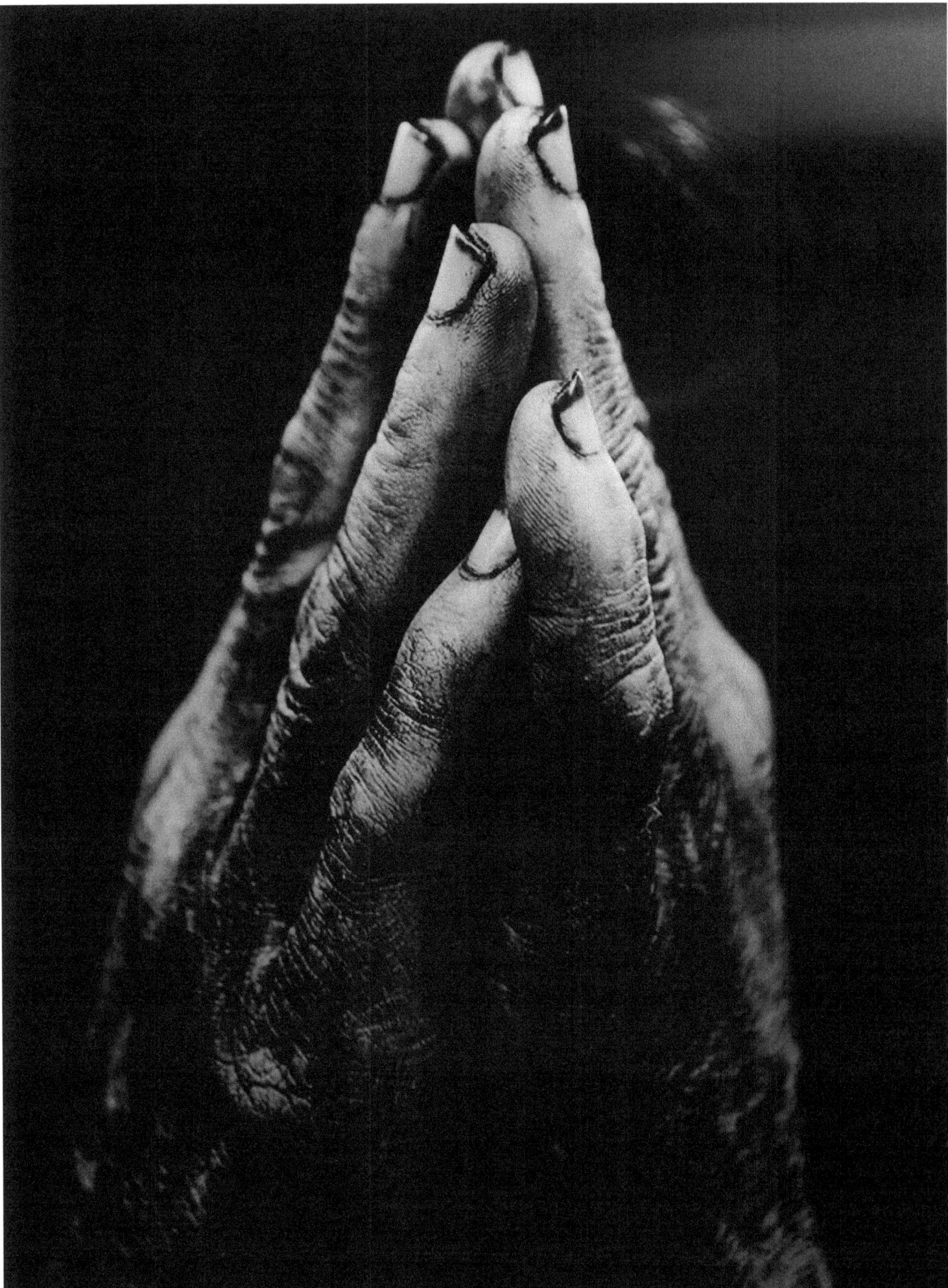

BECAUSE EVEN HERE, GOD CAN BE FOUND.

HERE I AM - PART 1
Available

Jesse (husband) and I had been through some difficult times over the course of a few years. Uncertainty, pain, heartache, loss... it was challenging. But at the same time, we found beauty in the mess: as much as we deconstructed, we reconstructed, too. We made huge plans and hopes and ideas for ourselves, our gorgeous kids, our incredible Pocket Fuel community and beyond. For the first time in years, I felt emotionally and spiritually excited and ready to go for 'it,' whatever 'it' may be.

But while navigating that new place of freedom we'd found ourselves in, I couldn't throw myself full, because just as I was rising out of the ashes, my health took a blow. On the one hand, I was excited and hopeful and full of life. On the other, exhausted and frustrated and almost ready to give up.

That's when I decided to do what I'd wanted to do since my parents told me I couldn't:

I got my first tattoo.

On the inside of my left arm just below my elbow, in a handwritten cursive style, are the words:

Here I am.

The ancient Hebrew word for that sentence is Hineni. It's a beautiful word used only a few times in the Biblical text, but each and every time, it was during moments of transition, transformation and hardship for those who uttered it.

I grew up being the biggest "pick me, Jesus" girl on the block. Perhaps even my whole town. I was at every service; I read my bible prolifically, I prayed, I started the prayer group at school. I even told all the kids in the Kindergarten that "Santa wasn't real and Jesus is!" I was fanatical and enthusiastic and desperate to be picked by God.

"Here I am?" I used to pray, petition, shout, scream. As if I was a kid on the sidelines waiting to be picked for the team. That's how I used to do Christianity. Here I am Lord, pick me! Because God might not. God might pick someone else.

But that's not what "here I am" means in its original Jewish sense. It's not "here I am" can you see me? It's "here I am" in this place, at this time, awake, aware and alive. Its a declaration of attention.

It's got nothing to do with being picked and sent and victorious. We are already those things (whatever they are and whatever they mean) without question, without even asking for them.

"Here I am" is the offer of total availability to what is happening in you and around you. It's how you answer when God calls.

We wait for the audible voice, the prophet or the preacher, the sage or the leader, the quickening of our spirit or heart, to hear the call of God. But I think God's always calling us to see and hear, to love and to take responsibility. God's whisper, and sometimes shout, can be heard through the different seasons of our lives: sickness, health, success, failure and everything in between; God's voice is in them all.

Did God cause my (or your) health challenges? I don't believe so. Not for a second. But I do know that the Divine was in it with me, calling me each day to be awake to presence even in the midst of pain and uncertainty.

So, I got it tattooed on my body: here I am. I am available to face what is going on in my life, with those I love, and in the world around me. No hiding, no running away: I am here.

Because even here, God can be found.

HERE I AM - PART 2
Whom Shall I Send?

When Abraham was called Abram and first heard the voice of God ask him leave home and journey to a new land (Gen 12); years later when God asked him to sacrifice his only son Isaac on an altar (Gen 22); In a dream about goats when Jacob was young (Gen 31) and then years later when he was older; when the bush burned right in front of Moses and then spoke to him (Ex 3); when Samuel heard the voice of God in the dead of night (1 Sam 3); When Isaiah saw the Lord in a vision, high and exalted, seated on a throne, the train of his robe filling the entire temple (Isa 6):

They all responded with:

Hineni.
Here I am.
Wide awake and available.

Of course, you could interpret the "here I am" of their responses to be a "Pick me, I'm over here Lord, I'll do the work, you can trust me..." type of thing. But for each of these humans, there was more going on than that.

Through the years, I've heard this verse preached particularly in the light of the sixth chapter of Isaiah when, during a vision, God asked:

"Whom shall I send? And who will go for us?"

And Isaiah replied,

"Here I am Lord, send me."

It's as if Isaiah had been waiting for the call of God with bated breath and was ready, desperate, and would go wherever he was sent and would say whatever he was told. (Side note: did you notice that God referred to Godself in plural terms? Nice, hey. Cos that's linear *note sarcasm*.) God then told Isaiah to go here and there and say this and that. And we can guess that he did what he was told.

Since the book of Isaiah has been preached, this verse has been used as a kind of warning, or standard: "When God calls, you answer, and what God says, you do! Whether you like it or not. You want to be ready when God calls! You want to be available! Listen, or you might miss it."

I've spent much of my life ready and waiting for the call. Which means I camped out at all the conferences waiting to hear all the big important speakers, I bought the books, wrote the emails, waited in lines, went out for prayer (so.much.prayer), waited to be prophesied over (is that still a thing?), read bible plans, went on retreats... I was ever waiting for that call.

And sure I heard it, I think, a bunch of times. To move here, and do that, and say certain words... But in a way, I was always waiting to have that "Whom shall I send? – Send ME!" with lightning-and-rainbows-and-wind-and-rain-and-sunshine-all-at-once moment. Like God would knight me or something, give me a sword and send me on my way, a recognized, chosen, I've-been-picked champion.

And it never happened. I said yes to things thinking I was saying yes to the call of God and in the end? It all fell apart.

You see, God wasn't asking those guys in the Biblical text "Where are you? I've got a special job for you." It just seems like that because of the way the story has been told for the last few hundred years.

In context, these men were on the verge of change, transformation, breaking the cultural rules, making hard decisions, decisions they had no precedents for. They were in the thick of their own lives wondering what to do. And they owned it. They showed up. They took responsibility. They stepped out. They committed to the transformation. They didn't run or hide or flee or escape. They said:

Here I am!

They picked themselves.

HERE I AM - PART 3
Rock Bottom

"Why does it always rain on me?

Is it because I lied when I was seventeen?"

Francis Healy went to Israel for a holiday so he could leave the rains of Scotland behind and enjoy some quality sunshine. But it rained from the moment he got off the plane to the moment he got back on. He wrote this song (the lines above) for his band Travis on the way home to try and cheer himself up.

Have you ever asked, why me? Why does it always seem to rain on me? Why does crap always seem to happen to me?

Do you compare yourself to others? Negatively? Why me and not them?

It's super easy to get caught in a "why me" loop. Especially when it seems like everyone else is trouble free. We look for something to blame, too: "Its not my fault." Or the "why me" loop morphs into an "I always do the wrong thing" downward spiral.

Why me? It must be because I'm defective. (Feeling encouraged yet?)

You know what? No one is trouble free. I'm dealing with something, you're dealing with something else, and someone we don't know is dealing with something else entirely, and we can all say "Why me," feel alone, hard done by, and like it isn't fair. And perhaps it's not fair. What's happening in your life, mine, and your neighbors could be the furthest thing from fair that there is.

But where you are is where you are. Whether you got yourself there, or not. It is what it is. Which can be the most defeated thing to say or the most powerful thing to say.

Before I get ahead of myself, let me say this: comparison will do you no favors. That girl on Instagram, that guy at the office, the person driving the taxi, the woman behind the counter, your best friend a town away; they may not be going through what you are. But they are going through something, or least have before and will again. Let that be a source of solidarity. Your circumstances may be unique, but the fact that you struggle is not.

The "why me?" question is one that we all ask. But it's not a question we should cling to.

"Here I am" has been my antidote to "why me?" It's my "this is where I am, right here at this moment, with this stuff going on, and these resources." It helps me face it, be present in it for what it is, no comparisons, no hiding, no "why me." Owning it. Offering my total availability.

For the Biblical characters mentioned in the last post, this was their "here I am" – total availability and responsibility to what was happening – not "I'm over here, pick me."

As one of my literary heroes, JK Rowling, said: *"Rock bottom became the solid foundation on which I rebuilt my life."* (1.)

Here I am. In this. On this. Exactly as it is. And I'm ready to work with it.

So if you've hit rock bottom, overall or in a certain situation, it's okay. Even if it seems like it's raining a lot right now, you can do this. Instead of focusing on "why me?" and comparing yourself to everyone else's highlight reels, look yourself in the mirror and say:

Here. I. Am.

There's power in that admission.

HERE I AM - PART 4

Taking Responsibility

Responsibility is at the heart of the phrase: "Here I am."

Hineni (the ancient Hebrew word for "here I am") isn't about being picked or chosen or sent. It's about listening and seeing and taking responsibility.

After Abraham had said "hineni," he went on to establish a new tribe and a new way of seeing God (more on that in future series).

When Jacob said "hineni," he wrestled with God, had his name changed, and his children birthed the twelve tribes of Israel.
When Moses said "hineni," he went on to set his people free after four hundred or more years of slavery in Egypt.
When Samuel said "hineni," he went on to become one of the first great prophets of Israel. And what does a prophet do? Speak truth to power.
When Isaiah said "hineni," he went on to become what many believe to be the greatest prophet of Israel, and like above, what does a prophet do?

These weren't puppets being sent to do a job.

These guys took responsibility for what was happening in them and around them. Here I am, in this political climate, with this health condition, with these people struggling over here, and those people waging war over there. Here I am, eyes open, ears listening, heart soft.

"Live creatively, friends. If someone falls into sin, forgivingly restore him, saving your critical comments for yourself. You might be needing forgiveness before the day's out. Stoop down and reach out to those who are oppressed. Share their burdens, and so complete Christ's law. If you think you are too good for that, you are badly deceived.

Make a careful exploration of who you are and the work you have been given, and then sink yourself into that. Don't be impressed with yourself. Don't compare yourself with others. Each of you must take responsibility for doing the creative best you can with your own life." Paul, Gal 6:1-5 (MSG).

There are so many saying "It's not my problem" in our world.

Climate change? Excessive waste? Garbage filled ocean? Food quality decline? Not my problem.
Over crowded prisons? Sentencing injustices? Support for victims? Rehabilitation for offenders? Not my problem.
Racism? Misogyny? Gender equality? Equality for all? Not my problem.
We have people who have more money than they'll ever need, and people who can't afford what they need, but hey... "not my problem."

But it is.

Here I am, here we are, in the midst of all of this.

Put on this earth, at this time, for this moment. God calls to us through all of life, the good and the bad. God pulls on our hearts and bends our ears and burns our eyes with it all so that we would "make a careful exploration of who we are and the work we've been given, and then sink ourselves into that."

To say "here I am" is to take responsibility for the things happening in you and around you.

You are not powerless; you are not weak (even if you feel it). God called an old man (Abraham), a deceiving son (Jacob), a crazy wilderness wanderer (Moses), a child (Samuel), and weird, outspoken guy (Isaiah) – ordinary, normal folk. We only think they were extra special because we can read about them hundreds and thousands of years after their story was first told.

But they were just people who opened their eyes and woke up and did what they could.

And we can all do that.

When you start saying "here I am" to your life, it has a way of saying it back.

HERE I AM - PART 5

Send Me

The vision of Isaiah and his "here I am, Lord" moment could be one of the most well-known stories in faith communities (found in Isaiah 6).

But something interesting happens in Isaiah 52:

"Early on, my people went to Egypt and lived, strangers in the land. At the other end, Assyria oppressed them. And now, what have I here?"

God's Decree.

"My people are hauled off again for no reason at all. Tyrants on the warpath, whooping it up, and day after day, incessantly, my reputation blackened. Now it's time that my people know who I am, what I'm made of—yes, that I have something to say. Here I am!" (Isa 52:4-6).

Here I am is a two-way street. A "draw near to God and he will draw near to you" (James 4:8) type thing. When we show up for our lives, it's as if the Divine shows up, too. God's been there all along of course, but in that moment of awareness and wakefulness, it's as if we feel God more closely. Some call it aligment, others call it flow.

Whatever you're saying "hineni" to today, know that the Divine, the creator of all things, the essence and power that got this whole started, unconditional love, says it right back.

To your pain, your joy, your challenge, your responsibility, your heartache, your power, your sense of purpose, your anger and fear and doubt and longing and laughter and outrage; all the stuff going on in the world today, the good, the bad, the ugly, the outrageous, the unfair, the beautiful, the holy, and the mess;

God offers his total availability to any and all who would have it. The Divine says:

Here I am.

Even in the midst of this.

HERE I AM - PART 6
Showing Up To Your Life

Hineni.

This ancient word has been saving my life. Its helped me take responsibility not only for me, but the stuff going on around me, too. It doesn't matter whether or not we're directly culpable, to blame, or if the mess belongs to us. If there's mess, and we can see it, let's do something about it. If there's joy and we can touch it, let's hug the life out of it. If there's wonder and we can feel it, let's let it tingle up and down our spines and thrill us.

Because that old cliché is true: all we have is now, and our agency to do with it whatever we choose.

To say "here I am" is to surrender. No running, no hiding. A gracious and humble showing up for whatever is going on in you and around you.

And look, there's a lot going on, right? Sometimes, you have to choose what get's your availability. But your body, spirit, and heart will help you navigate it all.

When you start saying "here I am" to your life, it has a way of saying it back. It's a grace. Listen to Spirit, it'll lead you through.

There's no better way to show up for own lives than by showing up for others. Sometimes (I think most) they are so entwined you can't tell them apart.

"What I'm interested in seeing you do is: sharing your food with the hungry, inviting the homeless poor into your homes, putting clothes on the shivering ill-clad, being available to your own families. Do this and the lights will turn on, and your lives will turn around at once. Your righteousness will pave your way. The God of glory will secure your passage. Then when you pray, God will answer. You'll call out for help and I'll say, 'Here I am."
- Isaiah 58:7-9 (MSG).

"Rock bottom became the solid foundation on which I rebuilt my life." — JK Rowling

"IT IS NOT ENOUGH TO SAY PRAYERS; ONE MUST BECOME, BE PRAYER, PRAYER INCARNATE."

Paul Evodkimov

"I am a gem, as are you, with many facets. We can't be figured out in a glance. The more you think you know, the more you realise there is yet more to know."

BEYOND THE LABEL - PART 1
Seventy Faces

In the Rabbinic Tradition, it is said that there are at least seventy facets or faces to each word of scripture. Just like a gem or a diamond, you have to turn it to see all the beauty found in each facet and face. Each turn reveals something different from the last. That's where the beauty of a diamond is found: one can sparkle in many different ways. We know there is a single light within the stone, but we see that light differently depending on the face we're looking at, and in which light, and on what angle. One diamond becomes seventy different diamonds as it turns (1).

"There is a divine intention underlying every text (scripture). But we cannot completely grasp that with our finite minds. Therefore, we search out the meaning of the text in order to draw closer to the divine meaning – freed from the constraints of trying to find one correct meaning. Narratives by their very nature are multivalent; they have many meanings that touch different levels of our lives and address different issues brought by the hearer of the story. Too often religious communities assign one meaning or moral to the story and close out the other, deeper, truer possibilities." Explained H. Stephen Shoemaker (2).

It's the same for our lives. It's easy to read one line on Twitter or Instagram and instantly sum up a person/project/organisation/issue: affix the label and move on. We do it offline, too. Maybe even more so.

But life is more complicated than that. We are more vast than that. I am a gem, as are you, with many facets. I can't be figured out in a five-minute reading (thirty-six years on and I can still be a mystery to myself). You are not two dimensional and easy to define. Neither is Scripture. The more you dive in, the more you realise there is yet to know. And in the same way that pressure creates precious stones, when we apply the pressure of questions and context and more to the scriptures, they don't crumble... more beauty is revealed.

The seventy facets or faces used metaphorically in the Rabbinic tradition of reading scripture (mentioned above) is kind of like when Peter asked Jesus how many times he should forgive, and Jesus said seventy times seven as a way of saying "however many times it takes." It's not actually four hundred and ninety – it's a nondescript number: open and unending.

In the (modern) Christian tradition, we read the Parables of Jesus (and scripture in its entirety) as if they're allegories, with one flat undisputed meaning. But they're not allegories. They don't have one hidden meaning. Parables were (traditionally) designed and used to shake up one's worldview, to question the conventional, to reveal the hidden stuff in hearts and lives, and to keep people on their social, political, relational, and theological toes.

"We read it, and we let it read us. We dive into their story, discovering our story in the process," said Rob Bell of parables (3).

With that and the seventy faces of Scripture in mind, let's "turn the gem" of the Parable of the Persistent Widow. Her story only lasts a few lines, and it seems straightforward, simple, easy. Luke wrote that:

"Jesus told them a story showing that it was necessary for them to pray consistently and never quit." (Luke 18:1 MSG.)

Straight up, we know this is a parable about connection, flow, openness, and awareness (all the things that prayer is).

But what are we to be aware of?

BEYOND THE LABEL - PART 2
What Faithfulness Could Be

Luke said that Jesus told this story to show people that they should pray consistently and never give up:

"In a certain city there was a judge who neither feared God nor had respect for people. In that city there was a widow who kept coming to him and saying, 'Grant me justice against my opponent.' For a while he refused; but later he said to himself, 'Though I have no fear of God and no respect for anyone, yet because this widow keeps bothering me, I will grant her justice, so that she may not wear me out by continually coming." (Luke 18:2-5 TJANT.)

Yep. That's it. That's the story meant to teach us how to be unwavering in prayer.

One city.
Two people.
A nasty judge.
A justice-seeking widow.
Justice granted because "leave me alone, thank you very much."

I've been taught this parable since childhood, and it's never made a lot sense to me. I get it (kind of) from the widows perspective: she wanted justice, and she didn't give up. But the way the Judge's character has been portrayed by preachers and teachers has never sat well.

If we're going to treat this story as an allegory, which is the popular interpretation amongst Pentecostals and Evangelicals, the widow is us, her cry for justice is our prayer, and there is no other character for the judge to be than God. But Jesus made a point of saying that the judge had no fear of God and no respect for people. I don't think the allegory works.

It starts to get a little more interesting and challenging when we treat this story like it's meant to be: a parable, and we dig into the Jewishness of it. We know that it's intended to disrupt us, make us think, and feel uncomfortable because that's what a parable is meant to do. We know there must be a hook, or a trick in there somewhere; it's too easy otherwise. Let's turn the gem of this multifaceted story... what else could it be saying to us?

For starters, forget the heading. The NIV translation has it as: "The Parable of the Persistent Widow." It was added centuries after Luke wrote his memoir, and does nothing but throw us off the scent of the meaning of the parable.

This is what we know for sure about the story:

It's meant to stir things up.
It's about prayer and tenacity.
It's about a widow and a judge and an answered cry for help (or is it... more on that later).

The strangest part of the parable are the words Jesus said after he finished the story:

"Listen to what the unjust judge says. And will not God grant justice to his chosen ones who cry to him day and night? Will he delay long in helping them? I tell you, he will quickly grant justice to them. And yet, when the Son of Man comes, will he find faith on earth?" (Luke 18:6-8 TJANT.)

It's about being faithful.

Verse six and seven are nice and comforting and make me feel good, but verse eight? What does that have to do with our story about prayer, a widow, a judge, and justice?

Perhaps, first of all, we should let go of our preconceived ideas of what prayer, widows, judges, and justice look like. Because after all, when Jesus spoke about justice, he often said weird things like love your enemies, do good to those who do wrong by you... he spoke about compassion and forgiveness and grace and love. He opposed an unjust justice system and was murdered for it. If we can sink into these ideas for a moment, or forever, we might start to see what faithfulness could be.

There could be more going on in this parable than we think...

BEYOND THE LABEL - PART 3
Your Whole Life is a Prayer

Prayer is not something we do, it's something we are a part of. It's more than words and phrases and knees on floors and heads bowed. Prayer means God is here and we are connected to God. It's being awake, aware, and alive to the Divine around, in, and through us.

"It is not enough to say prayers; one must become, be prayer, prayer incarnate." Said Paul Evodkimov. *"It is not enough to have moments of praise. All of life, each act, every gesture, even the smile of the human*

face, must become a hymn of adoration, an offering, a prayer. One should offer not what one has, but what one is." (4.)

Your whole life is a prayer.

"And there was a widow in that town who kept coming to him with the plea, 'Grant me justice against my adversary.'" (Luke 18:3 NIV.)

When we think of those who are vulnerable, and in need, our mind often goes to widows and orphans. And rightly so. All through the scriptures are decrees and commands that they are to be cared for, supported and included. And rightly so.

But some of the most resilient, strong, gutsy, resourceful, wise people I know are those who society would label as vulnerable and in need of 'care.' I'm all for caring, but sometimes caring feels more like patronising; putting people in boxes, treating them how we think they need to be treated rather than listening to what they want and really need, or noticing what they can do and can contribute, or including them and their voice in the current conversation.

Just because a woman is a widow doesn't mean she's weak. We come to this scripture with an assumption about what the label "widow" means. We assume that a widow is someone who needs to be aided rather than emulated. Perhaps this is where the challenge of our parable begins...

"Biblical widows are the most unconventional of conventional figures." Explains Amy Jill Levine. "Expected to be weak, they move mountains; expected to be poor, they prove savvy managers; expected to be exploited, they take advantage where they find it." (5.)

Women (widows) like:

Tamar (Gen 38:11).
Naomi (1 Sam 27:3).
Ruth (1 Sam 30:5).
The wise woman of Tekoa (2 Sam 14:5).
Judith of Bethulia.
And more...

They all manifest agency and defy the convention of the poor and dependant woman who could only ever "need."

In ancient Judaism women were not completely powerless, they did have rights and could employ them when needed. Our widow may not have been a helpless woman with no options. There is nothing in the parable to suggest that. In fact, she may have been the exact opposite.

She lived in a city: a place where you wouldn't normally find a destitute widow. She continually badgered the judge, which means that she had the time and means to do so. In the original text, the judge isn't concerned that the widow will wear him out, he's scared that she'll 'give [him] a black eye.' Yep. And was it for justice? Or vengeance that she continually showed up? We don't know. The story doesn't say. And that's part of the challenge.

The widow in Luke 18:1-8 may have been destitute, abused, desperate, and her actions towards the judge her last and final chance of survival. Or she could have been well off, powerful, and vengeful. Or perhaps she was somewhere in between. But if we stereotype her, approach the story with assumptions and labels, we can ignore the challenge of the parable, and in turn, ignore how it challenges our stereotypes.

What if part of prayer is to be aware of our tendency to stereotype people and situations? What if prayer is the challenge to listen a little longer and look a little harder beyond our labels and biases?

≈

BEYOND THE LABEL - PART 4
Turning the Gem

"There was a judge in a certain city," he said, "who neither feared God nor cared about people." Luke 18:2 (TJANT.)

If the judge had no respect for the Divine and was indifferent towards others, why are we so quick to think he is a metaphor for God in this short parable Jesus told?

N.B.: if something doesn't make sense in scripture, don't ignore it. It's most likely written that way deliberately to spike your curiosity so that you'll lean into it, dig into the meaning, question it till you find something you can sink your teeth into. The ancients were not ignorant idiots. Their writing style is full of humour, satire, and hyperbole; all used to cause the reader and the hearer to think, question, and be challenged. We need to keep "turning the gem" of scripture (as discussed in Part 1 of this series), to see its many layers and faces.

Back to our parable: The judge doesn't make a good metaphor for God. He doesn't care about people. He doesn't fear the divine. He is independent and narcissistic; in it for his own purposes, or at least, not for the sake of justice.

In our day and age, many of us marvel at the sentences and decisions of judges and the people in control of our legal system. A lot of the time, the justice system seems to be the institution least concerned with justice in our society. Perhaps not much has changed since the days of Jesus. We have to ask: what is justice?

It's believed that Ghandi said:

"An eye for an eye makes the whole world blind..."

For many of us, the idea of relying on the justice system to provide justice is as weak a dependancy as relying on chocolate to provide us with good health. I don't want to dishonour the system, but it's not a new phenomenon that the justice system sometimes seems to skip the justice part.

The judge in Jesus short story had no intention of granting the widow her request: "For a while he refused...(Luke 18:4)."

What was her request? A more correct translation of the original language suggests that the widow wasn't actually seeking justice. Rather, what she sought was vengeance (6). She wanted the judge to avenge her, make her opponent pay up. What makes the judge finally give in? Was it the widows tenacity? Her persistence? Or her threat of violence?

Jesus said that the judge thought to himself: "Though I have no fear of God and no respect for anyone, yet because this widow keeps bothering me, I will grant her justice, so that she may not wear me out by continually coming."

In the original Greek, the judge isn't worried that the widow will "wear him out" as in make him tired, but will give him a "black eye." (6, again.)

Whether or not a judge should fear physical violence from a widow is something you might question, but that in and of itself challenges our default to stereotype and label individuals. We read Jesus short parable and think: widow = vulnerable and weak, judge = upright and Godly. But in this parable, these figures don't fall in line with our typical stereotypes. They defy the conventional, they turn our labels upside down. The story begs us to see the individual rather than the group we would categorise them in.

Jesus was brilliant at this; he continually took figures that we would put in one box and displayed them acting outside of it. Our labels don't work. Not then, and not now.

We have to think outside the box.

Or perhaps think (and pray) as if there is none...

BEYOND THE LABEL - PART 5
Standing Up for Justice

In its original context, the widow was not seeking 'justice' as we might perceive... the word originally used more closely translates to 'vengeance.' Perhaps our widow was not the vulnerable, helpless woman seeking justice, but rather a shrewd and canny lady seeking vengeance who would go to violent means to get it.

But hang on... would a widow, a poor defenceless woman, who needs our care and support, seek vengeance? And threaten violence? When we shake down the stereotypes we bring to this parable, we can really dig into the story. If this story is about justice, we have to ask:

What does justice look like for Jesus?
That someone pays their debt?
That a wrong is made right?
That the offending party is made accountable for their actions?
For Jesus, is the court the place where you'll find justice? And when Jesus promises justice, what does that mean for those we seek justice from? And what about the justice they seek, too?

Jesus spoke about peace and grace and compassion. Forgiveness and freedom and redemption. He defended the woman who should have been stoned for adultery. He challenged his followers to pray for their Roman oppressors. He ate with tax collectors and sex workers - those culturally unaccepted; he healed people without asking whether or not they deserved it. He never used violence to exact justice. In fact, he peacefully submitted himself to an unjust legal system that manipulated every right that he had and murdered him for no other reason than religious animosity. His message threatened their control and sense of security.

It's not that we should let people walk all over us, that we should never seek justice; that people shouldn't be made accountable for their actions. But if we lived in a world where justice was extracted for everything done to us, and everything we've done to others, we would all owe a debt we could never repay.

In the parable, the judge didn't grant the widow justice because he thought it was the right thing to do. He did it because he didn't want to be beaten up and bothered.

Was the widow justified in her accusations and demands? Was she right to threaten the judge with violence to get what was owed her? I'm not judging her for that! If someone were to hurt my family or shortchange someone I love, I would want to seek vengeance, too.

This is the hook and challenge of this parable. And perhaps that's why at the outset, Luke said that it was about our need to pray continually. In a world bent on getting what it thinks it deserves, on vengeance, an eye for an eye; someone somewhere has to stop the cycle. Someone has to forgive. And if that's not the message of the cross, I don't know what is.

"All the figures in the parable, and we readers as well, have become enmeshed in, if not colluded with, this system set up at best for a "justice" whose legitimacy is never determined, revenge that by any other name constitutes vengeance. The problem is not ultimately the court. The court is only a system of the larger systemic concern: the human desire for vengeance, a desire that knows no gender or class boundaries, a desire that sucks everyone into its wake. Thus true systemic evil is revealed—and of course readers seek to deny it." (7.)

What does that mean for us?

It means we pray. We pay attention to Spirit, we submit ourselves to grace and redemption. We ask for forgiveness, and we give it, too. Or at least, we work on it. We stand up for justice, always. But at some point, we have to make a decision about what Godly justice looks like, feels like, and tastes like. We have to extract vengeance from our sense of it.

That could be what Jesus meant when he finished the parable and said:

"And yet, when the Son of Man comes, will he find faith on earth?"

IF YOU ONLY STICK TO LABELS, YOU'LL NEVER FIND THE TRUTH.

BEYOND THE LABEL - PART 6
Labels and Truth

Every single day in a thousand different ways, tragedy, terror, hatred and violence fill up the space between souls. On a more subtle and less tangible level, we hold our differences up against each other like barriers, convinced of our separateness. Convinced of our personal "rightness." Convinced that we are owed. And we'll do anything to make sure we get it.

"Labels are like material possessions: they are necessary, but we don't need to give them as much meaning as we often do." Said The Minimalists (8).

Our brains receive up to six billion bits of information PER SECOND! (yep.) But cognitively, we can only process around three thousands bits of information per second. Labels help us file all this information in our brains efficiently, but they get tricky when we rely on them too heavily. There is always more to a person, a story, life, culture, religion, then the attached label.

Our great challenge as humans trying to live the best we can in this crazy, beautiful, multifaceted world, where we believe in free speech and freedom of religion and the right to be treated with dignity, is to live beyond our labels of each other. Dig into them. Find out the story, the detail, the personality, the situations, and circumstances. There is so much MORE to me and you and our lives individually and collectively than the labels we get filed under in the minds of others, and the labels we file others under, and the labels we file ourselves under.

'Christian' is a label that can be applied to me, stuck to my chest with my name neatly printed underneath. But it's a label I sometimes loathe to wear. To be honest, there are some who share this label with me, yet we share little else – our faith and lives and ideas and values and stories and practices couldn't be further from each other. But if you only stick to labels, you'd never know.

You have to get interested in what's under the label. What lives and breathes and moves in the blood, bone, and breath of a human.

We have to ask: is there more to the widow, the judge, and justice, than their labels? And what do we do when we find out what that something 'more' is?

That's why we need to be faithful to prayer; being awake, aware and alive to the presence of God in us and others. Why we need to challenge ourselves to dig deeper than stereotypes, and perhaps dig deeper when we want revenge; try and find something else to finish the story with.

Is this parable about the Widow and the Judge a subversive tale of labels and justice, to keep on praying and be faithful?

Or is it that if an unjust judge can grant the weakest-of-the-weak favour, how much more so will the Divine who is just grant all of us justice?

Perhaps as we turn the gem of scripture in the different lights of our lives and seasons, it's both.

YOU ARE WHERE YOU ARE,
SO BE THERE. ALL THERE.

WHAT'S NEXT - PART 1
The Wonder of it All

Finally, all was quiet.

Noise gave way to smell and sight. Light broke through the cracks in the walls, dust danced in its rays, and if you followed a single speck, you'd see it land on the baby asleep in his mother's arms.

He smelt as new as the first day.

Blood and wine lingered in the air, she could still taste it... the sweet and bitter mix. Some time had passed since her bloodied clothes and ruined tunic had been taken away, and the thick red stains had been washed from her skin. But as with all women who birth life from their bodies, blood still flowed from her emptying womb. What was once one, was now two but still somehow joined in a new way that she could only describe as holy.

Yes, that's it, she thought as she picked at the salt beneath her nails.

As soon as he was free of her body, the cord that joined them had been severed. They had washed him with wine and water, anointed him with oil and salt, wrapped him, and laid him in her arms. Where he'd been ever since.

This new and holy bond was more powerful than she'd imagined: it threatened to rip her heart in pieces and fill it up with joy all at the same time.

She kissed his head. He stirred and nuzzled into her chest: eyes squinting, mouth working, looking for sustenance. Her breasts swelled with milk as she pulled the blankets open and fed her newborn baby.

There in the dark, her mind went back to the birth. There had more blood than she expected. And more pain. Goodness, the pain had been unbearable, but in a miraculously bearable kind of way.

During the pregnancy, she'd often wondered what this particular birth would be like. She had seen women in labour before, even assisted the midwives when her mother was in labour with her younger brothers and sisters. She knew what to expect.

Yet still, she had wondered if his birth would be different? Would there be blood? Pain? What does one expect when giving birth to the Messiah?

Of course, she never talked about it. Never asked any questions. She couldn't. As it was, she was endlessly questioned about her swelling belly. She and Joseph had not yet been married when the baby started to grow inside her, and she'd wanted to quiet the scandal as much as possible and save what was left of her dignity. And that of her father's.

Still, she had silently wondered, doubted, questioned... had the Angel really visited her? Was what he said true? Was there any way she could know for sure?

Now, in this dimly lit room, Joseph asleep beside her, her new child - Oh! This promised, miraculous child - drinking his fill from her, she was struck by the humanity of it all. It was absolutely, utterly Divine.

She held a secret in her arms. A hidden promise, a vulnerable hope. A soft laugh escaped her lips, and her body shuddered. Even though she had climbed down from the heights of pain, it still thudded through her; a reminder of the power of her own flesh.

Her own body. God's own son.

Ridiculous.
Unbelievable.
Holy.

What now?

How would they raise this child? What was Joseph feeling? Where would they live? Should they tell people? Or keep this secret hidden away in their hearts to be revealed in time? Perhaps the Angel would visit again and tell them what to do next?

But there in the darkness, the day after she gave birth to the boy they had already called Jesus though his naming day had not yet come, Mary pushed the fear aside, at least for now, and smiled at the wonder of it all.

"Learn from yesterday, live for today, hope for tomorrow." — Einstein

WHAT'S NEXT - PART 2
Do Not Yield To Your Fear

What do you do the day after the day you've been waiting for your whole life?

What comes next?

All this waiting and focus and expense and preparation spent on a single event or day… what happens when it's all over? What do you find in the aftermath? What do you do with it? Do you move on straight away? Do you sit and dream about what has been?

I wonder if Mary felt that those days and weeks after the birth of Jesus were a bit of an anti-climax… Motherhood settling in: sleepless nights, repairing body, tired mind and heart. She had just given birth to the Messiah as the Angel foretold she would, and she had prepared for her God-Son for months.

But then the day came. And just like all the days before it, it ended. Time moves at a steady pace, unaware of our events and moments – the ones we want to hold onto and the ones we want to speed by in an instant. It keeps moving forward as always, regardless.

When the Angel first appeared to Mary, it told her:

"Do not yield to your fear." (Luke 1:30 TPT.) Something was about to happen, yes. An event was coming, yes. She was to prepare for it, yes. But then, as always, there was life after and beyond it.

Don't let fear *rule* you.

This horrific or successful moment/day/year/event you've just experienced will come to an end, as all things must.

What do you do next?

First step: Don't surrender to fear. There is more life in store for you. There's more growth, there's more to learn, more to do and more to be. There's more to pass on to others, there's more rest to heal you, more work to invigorate you, more generosity to humble you, and more grace to empower you.

But be here now. Live this moment all the way through. Bask in its sunset. And then, as the dawn comes, get up, and press on.

WHAT'S NEXT - PART 3
In the In-between

I wonder what's next for you?

What are you moving on from? Do you have an idea of where you're headed?

How do you transition from one thing – perhaps the very best event/year/moment/day, or the very worst – to the other side of it?

I've had high moments and hellish ones. Life just keeps moving on through it all, despite it all. It doesn't wait for me to catch up. There has always been, and always will be twenty-four hours in a day, seven days in a week, fifty-two weeks in a year. I can't change time. I can't hold it back, speed it up, or slow it down. But I can learn how to flow with it.

Letting go of what has been, or at least moving with the passing of time from an event, whether it was good or bad, is a skill we spend our lives working on (or not). It's the spaces between the big moments that are hard to navigate. Even in the initial moments of tragedy and heartache, there's stuff to do; things to plan, forms to fill out, people to call... it's the days, weeks and months afterward that are the hardest. Sometimes letting go can't come quick enough, and other times we hold onto old moments for dear life.

And all the while day follows night follows day follows...

The in-between time. One of the hardest, and yet, one of the most formative seasons we frequent. While we can't skip ahead to the next event, or wish the hard times away, the in-between time is where we actually do our best work, or at least have the potential to.

It's tempting to want to speed time up, slow it down, rush through it, sleep through it, numb through it... and get to the other side. But we risk losing the lessons and stories the in-between has for us.

So, just wait. Have a seat. Take a breath. Make that a few deep breaths.

The Bible doesn't tell us much about Mary's life, and nothing at all while Jesus was between the ages of twelve and thirty. Was this her in-between? Or were there a series of them we don't know anything about? The Angel appeared to her in the dead of night, told her she would have a baby who would be the Saviour of the world, AND that she would conceive without having sex... (Luke 1:26-38). And then she had to wait. Live through it ALL. Day by day, moment by moment. Grace by grace.

It's not a passive waiting; it's more of an active patience. Presence. You are where you are, so be there. All there. The Divine is at work in the in-between, weaving God's grand story through your life the way only God can, and only if we choose to be present in it.

If you're in the "in-between;" if it's the day after the day you've waited your whole life for, or feared your whole life, well then, this is where you are. Is it painful? Is it boring? Is it "whatever?" Joyful? Normal? Crazy? Whatever it may be, wake up. Get out of bed (figuratively and physically). Make yourself a coffee (tea, juice, smoothie...), and breathe into this day. Don't rush it, don't waste it by wishing it away. Even in the in-between – the aftermath, the day after the Big Day – we have no idea what's next... not in ten minutes or ten years. So we may as well put one foot in front of the other, and trust that more awaits us.

≈

"Don't surrender to fear. There is more life in store for you. There's more growth, there's more to learn, more to do and more to be."

WHAT'S NEXT - PART 4
Moving Forward

Trust is a tough one. It takes a long time to build and can be lost in a single moment. It's risky. It's uncertain (hence its nature...). We could lose a lot, maybe even everything.

But what's the alternative to "trusting?"

Romans 8:24 says:

"But hope means that we must trust and wait for what is still unseen" (TPT).

If hope means waiting and trusting, trust means faith and grace. It's the belief that there is more going on here than there is evidence for, and employing grace and boldness to search it out. It's vital for the in-between moments of life where we're asking "what's next?"

I wonder if Mary doubted her encounter with the Angel? I can imagine her questioning it in the middle of the hard times, like when they were refugees in Egypt, and she watched her son – the promised Saviour – die the most painful death possible on a Roman cross charged as a terrorist and an enemy of the state. Was God breaking trust with her? Did she waver in her trust of God?

If Mary was anything like me – and I'm going to take a wild guess and say that she may have been; we are both humans – then I would say, yep, she wavered. Big time. How could she have continued to trust God while watching the blood and life slowly leak out of her son's body?

But that's what trust does.

It doubts, it asks questions; it sobs and cries and screams, it drinks too much coffee, it meditates and prays... it waits. It hopes.

It engages the in-between – the day after the Big Day, the aftermath of tragedy or glory – with the belief that there is still more to come.

Yes, trust is easily broken. The temptation to trust less and less, the longer we live and the more experiences we have, is huge. And with some people, you need to be wise with your trust. But with the Divine? With life? The great challenge is to KEEP ON trusting, to keep our hearts and minds OPEN, and to believe that there is more going on here than we know.

It's easy to think Mary's questions and doubts from the Cross would have been answered with her son's resurrection… but think again. The people believed, and the Angel told her, that Jesus would rule over the house of Jacob (Luke 1). They thought the coming Messiah would win back their freedom, conquer Rome, and see their land returned.

But as we read in scripture, Jesus ascended into the Heavens having achieved none of that.

Did Mary and Jesus' followers still trust him? Were they disappointed? Did they feel abandoned and betrayed?

Do you? When things don't work out the way you thought they would, or if you feel like there is nothing left for you to do?

And yet as hard as it is, trust is what we need right now. Trust will get us out of bed in the morning. It's going to keep us engaged and telling our story. It's going to whisper in our ears: "you can do it, keep on going…" and yell in our faces: "You can do hard things." It's going to figure out how we can move forward, because, before there's any evidence of it being possible, it knows we can.

What's next? It could be any number of things.

Trust that through it all, God is not playing chess with your life, or the lives of others - God is present in every moment.

WHAT'S NEXT - PART 5
More to Come

What do you do the day after the day you've waited your whole life for? Or dreaded your whole life? What happens next?

What did Mary do, think and believe in the days after she gave birth to Jesus? As she fled to Egypt? When she lost him in the crowd only to find him at the temple? When he turned water into wine? As his influence and reputation swung like a pendulum from hero to villain (depending on who you talked to)? As he was beaten and tortured and hung on a cross as a terrorist and enemy of the state? As he came back to life with holes in his hands and side?

What's next after that?

Don't surrender to fear.
Wait.
Trust.
Hope.
There's more to come.

I'm not a huge fan of the saying, "The best is yet to come." How do I know that the best is ahead? How do you say that to a mother whose child has been given three months to live? Or a victim of abuse? The list goes on…

At its essence, this saying isn't about circumstantial "best," but I think we prescribe that to it.

We must remember that the best things in life are not things. They aren't even circumstances. Sure, I hope for better circumstances. I'd love a bigger house, better health, a nicer car, an easier job, more money, healthier self-esteem, a more functional family (love you guys)… but these things may never happen.

I may never get the "sorry" I deserve, the book deal I want, the promotion, the money, the house… maybe the "best" to come doesn't reside in those things.

Or in things at all.

And what about for those living in poverty? War? Refugees? The displaced? The homeless? Diseased? Betrayed? The falsely accused? Those rejected by communities? I cannot, and will not, throw them a catchy line like that. What they need are our ears and our willingness to see them and hear them. Solidarity, not platitudes.

Hope is a word, yes. But hope is tactile, too. It's made manifest through our eyes, hands, tables, homes, feet, ears, arms…

There is more to come. More life to be lived, more lessons to be learned, more love to give and receive, more mistakes to remind us of our humanity, and more grace to remind us of Divinity. There is more work to do, more sleep to have, more food to grow and make and distribute.

The sun is going to set tonight, and we'll say goodbye to the day. Tomorrow morning, the sun will rise again, and with it, a new day. Do what you need to – take the time to cherish the moments that changed you, mourn the ones that hurt you, take joy in the ones that thrilled you – do the work. And then…

What do you do now? What's next?

Who knows.

Meet it with all the love and grace and courage you have.

≈

YOUR TRUE BEING BRIMS OVER INTO TRUE WORDS AND DEEDS.

Luke 6:45 (MSG)

YOUR GOOD, GOOD HEART - PART 1
The Human Heart

Jeremiah said:

"Most devious is the heart; It is perverse – who can fathom it?" (Jeremiah 17:9 TJSB.)

The Psalmist said:

"Delight yourself in the Lord and he will give you the desires of your heart." (Ps 37:4 ESV.)

The writer of Proverbs said:

"Guard your heart above all else, for it is the source of life." (Prov 4:23 HSCB.)

Jesus said:

"For out of the heart come evil thoughts—murder, adultery, sexual immorality, theft, false testimony, slander." (Matt 15:19 NIV.)

But he also said:

"Blessed are the pure in heart, for they shall see God." (Matt 5:8 NIV.)

Paul said:

"For it is with your heart that you believe and are justified..." (Rom 10:10 NIV.)

In the entire Biblical Text, there are over seven hundred references to the heart that say all kinds of different things. Some condemn the heart, others seem to redeem it. Some make it sound like our hearts are docile and incapable of making good decisions, others suggest that our whole life is shaped by our heart.

So, which is it? Are our hearts fundamentally good or evil? Can they be trusted? Should we follow our heart? Listen to it? Pay attention to it?

With all the seemingly conflicting comments, commands, and directives about the human heart in the scriptures, I think we can conclude that the condition of our heart is of utmost importance. It's not that the heart IS evil or IS good but that our heart dictates the direction of our lives and can impact the path of others.

At the core of the matter is our heart itself. What's harbouring and happening in our heart is our truth. Good and bad, beautiful and ugly. I think it can be the case that at any given moment our hearts can be both positive and negative, sick and healing, broken and put back together.

The passage mentioned above in the book of Jeremiah goes on to say:

"The heart is hopelessly dark and deceitful, a puzzle that no one can figure out. But I, God, search the heart and examine the mind. I get to the heart of the human. I get to the root of things. I treat them as they really are, not as they pretend to be." (Jer 17:10 MSG.)

We judge people on a surface level: social media feeds, community demographics, personal economics, test scores, contribution, image... you get the idea. But God dives beyond the surface straight to the heart. God knows that our hearts are the foundation of our lives.

It's not that our hearts are good or evil. That's not the question. History tells us that the human heart has the capacity for both. The more interesting question is:

How do you keep a soft heart in a hard world? And can a soft heart change the world?

YOUR GOOD, GOOD HEART - PART 2
Hope for Us All

I was taught that my heart couldn't be trusted; it was evil, deceitful, dark. I was unworthy and undeserving of love and grace. I needed a Saviour to redeem me from the evil within and without that certainly had a firm grip on me.

Sounds grim, right? But that's what I believed. Maybe not so much on a conscious, daily, "these are my thoughts" level… but culturally? That's where I thought I stood in the world. Needless to say, these beliefs about my heart, amongst other things, cultivated other damaging beliefs and behaviours, too.

If my heart can't be trusted, what about others? If evil and darkness are at the foundation of my heart, what about others?

I was desperate to be made right, cured, and separated from my inner hell. I responded to multiple salvation calls (my collection of altar call bibles and tracts was impressive). I lived for approval and atonement. And I did not trust myself one bit. Emotions, desires, dreams, visions, plans… could I trust what came out of my heart? I was always waiting for "a word from God," which really means that for a long time (most of my late teens and twenties) I was immobile, undecided, still, stagnating. I would justify my condition by telling myself I was standing firm, holding to my convictions, being still in the presence of God. But truthfully? Making decisions was a nightmare.

What we believe about who and what we are drives our behaviour. The writer of Proverbs knew this when they wrote:

"So above all, guard the affections of your heart, for they affect all that you are. Pay attention to the welfare of your innermost being, for from there flows the wellspring of life." (Prov 4:23 TPT.)

What is at the heart of our heart? What you believe about the answer to that question affects all that you are, all that you do, and how you view others. We've been taught that we are inherently sinful; it's hardwired into our being. But what has been largely ignored and forgotten is that before the fall of humanity, before sin was a factor, at our very origin, God created us and said that we were… good.

Genesis begins the world with six clear statements of goodness. (Gen 1:10-31.) Original blessing is our truth, too.

Within each and every human being are threads of the Divine, the essence and source of life itself. We breathe it in and out every day and night – that first breath that God breathed into Adam, waking him up to life and beauty and goodness, sustains us all, still. I believe that goodness is our original design. If we seek it within ourselves, we'll find it.

"To say that the root of every person and creature is in God, rather than opposed to God, has enormous implications for how we view ourselves, and affects the way we view one another, even in the midst of terrible failings and falseness in our lives and world." Said John Philip Newell (1).

Instead of needing to be rescued from your heart, emancipated from your humanness, Christ invites you to be healed and restored to your true nature, which has been there all along. It's a homecoming, not a rescue mission. The core of your being is not in opposition to God but in harmony.

And if goodness is here among us, within us; if our hearts are indeed redeemable, healable, and restorable, there just might be hope for us all.

"Grace is given not to lead us into another identity but to reconnect us to the beauty of our deepest identity." —John Philip Newell

YOUR GOOD, GOOD HEART - PART 3
True Design

When Adam was formed of dust and spirit, God looked at God's creation and said that it was good. Goodness has been hardwired into our being from the very beginning. The deepest and most sacred parts of ourselves are not in opposition to God but in harmony. Sometime after our "birth," sin entered the scene, and has ever since damaged the heart of life, leaving pain and separateness in its wake. But sin was not part of our original design. We may be entangled in it, but it is not where we began.

That's not to say that sin isn't an issue. It is. Sin is simply the stuff that doesn't work; the stuff that stops us from growing, that leads to the death of love and hope and grace in our lives and relationships. Why did God command us not to commit adultery? Not to covet? Not to murder, and more? Because those things don't work for us, they don't lead to life.

John Scotus Eriugena, a ninth-century Irish Christian teacher, referred to sin as 'leprosy of the soul.' Just as leprosy distorts the human face and body, corroding its beauty and health beyond recognition, so sin distorts the heart. We've become so accustomed to the deformity, so used to living with the disease, that we believe it is our original and destined design.

Leprosy is a disease of insensitivity where you experience loss of feeling, and just like leprosy, sin leads us into insensitivity to what is deepest within us and each other. More and more we treat one another as if we are not made in the image of God. Instead of cooperating with each other, we compete. Significance is the goal, and we'll go to any length, even at the expense of others, to get it. Anything to make us feel better and hide our damage. From a personal to a national level, we hoard our abundance in fear that there won't be enough to go around.

Sin isn't God's kryptonite. God is not allergic to it, or even offended by it. The Divine can see what it does to our hearts. What it's always done: corrupt, corrode, growing over our true nature. The damage within comes out through our mouths and hands and feet; it shows in our words, actions, and policies; the things we are silent about and the things we scream about.

In ancient Hebrew tradition, the heart was the centre of someone's personhood; the seat of their emotions AND intelligence. Research conducted at the Heart Math Institute supports this ethos. They have discovered that the heart sends the brain 95% more signals than it receives from it. They believe that it's the heart, not the brain, that is the boss of our spiritual and physical beings (2).

Jesus said:

"Your true being brims over into true words and deeds." (Luke 6:45 MSG.)

He was reminding his listeners of the wisdom tradition:

"So above all, guard the affections of your heart, for they affect all that you are." (Proverbs 4:23.)

What's brimming over in our world? You don't have to look very far, perhaps not even beyond yourself, to see the damage, the leprous decay, festering in a world full of people who have forgotten who they really are.

But thankfully, as John Philip Newell says, *"Christ comes to reawaken us to our true nature"* (3).

≈

YOUR GOOD, GOOD HEART - PART 4
The Path to Healing

My therapist said to me almost every session:

"Hurting people hurt people."

I really do think that at the heart of it, it's that simple. When I examine my own heart, it's when I've been afraid, stressed, anxious, ashamed, threatened, hurt, and sometimes just plain hungry, that I lash out at others, be it those I love most, a group of people who are different from me and easy to blame for my inner rage, or just random citizens (road rage anyone?).

When my heart is compromised, my 'living' is too. This is why forgiveness is so radical, it changes everything. The sermon Jesus delivered on the Mount of Olives – which some scholars believe happened the week before he was betrayed by his own people and executed by the Romans – is a game changer in every way.

"Love your enemies. Let them bring out the best in you, not the worst. When someone gives you a hard time, respond with the energies of prayer. For then you are working out of your true selves, your God-created selves." Matt 5:44-45 (MSG.)

We love to quote it and smile about it and post it on social media, but rarely do we understand that that sermon - those words Jesus put out into the atmosphere - was deeply subversive and contrary and counterculture. It's no wonder they killed him.

In his speech, "Love Your Enemies," Martin Luther King said:

"The degree to which we are able to forgive determines the degree to which we are able to love our enemies." (4.)

It starts with you. With me. In our hearts. If hurting people hurt people, how can we heal the hurt within and without?

You are forgiven.
Forgive yourself.
Love the enemy that you have become to yourself.

Martin Luther King went on to say:

"We must recognise that the evil deed of the enemy-neighbour, the thing that hurts, never quite expresses all that he is. An element of goodness may be found even in our worst enemy. Each of us is something of a schizophrenic personality, tragically divided against ourselves. A persistent civil war rages within all our lives. Something within us causes us to lament with Ovid, the Latin Poet, "I see and approve the better things, but follow worse." Or to agree with Plato that human personality is like a charioteer having two headstrong horses, each wanting to go in a different direction. Or to repeat the Apostle Paul, "The good that I would I do not: but the evil which I would not, that I do." This simply means that there is some good in the worst of us and some evil in the best of us. When we discover this, we are less prone to hate our enemies. When we look beneath the surface, beneath the impulsive evil deed, we see within our enemy-neighbour a measure of goodness and know that the viciousness and evilness of his acts are not quite representative of all that he is. We see him in a new light. We recognise that his hate grows out of fear, pride, ignorance, prejudice, and misunderstanding, but in spite of this, we know God's image is ineffably etched into his being."

It starts in me and you. Behind every action is a story – our wounds and those of others. It doesn't excuse the behaviour, not one bit. It doesn't make an evil or hurtful act admissible. Not one bit. But it does shine a light on the path to healing. We'll never eradicate evil from the world by fighting it with evil.

"Hate cannot drive out hate, only love can do that." Martin Luther King (5).

YOUR GOOD, GOOD HEART - PART 5
Homecoming

I believe that the Christian tradition is less about re-locating my heart and spirit - grabbing a get out of hell free card, emancipating myself from the human condition - and more about finding and healing and owning and becoming.

For the ancient Hebrews, the heart was the centre of life. Everything a person did and was - emotion, intelligence, wisdom, consciousness: all heart. When the Biblical writers talk about having a pure heart, it doesn't mean a heart that behaves correctly and is without blemish, but rather a heart that is self-aware, and whole.

Cynthia Bourgeault said:

"In wisdom teaching, purity means singleness and the proper translation of this Beatitude [Blessed are the pure in heart for they shall see God. Matt 5:8] is, really, "Blessed are those whose heart is not divided" or "whose heart is a unified whole." Jesus emerged from his baptism as the ihidaya, meaning the "single one" in Aramaic." (6.)

The Biblical writers also speak of the false and stubborn heart; the heart distant from God. For them, a hypocrite was a person with a divided heart. Where we would say "two-faced," the Psalmist would say "two-hearted" (Ps 12:2-4).

That's why the heart can be both deceitful and pure. Why Jesus could say that out of the heart flows both goodness and evil. Why Paul said that it is by our hearts that we believe and are justified.

At the heart of the matter is the heart itself.

And this is perhaps the best news of all, because the heart? It's never beyond redemption.

Martin Luther King said: *"A persistent civil war rages within all our lives."* (7.)

God spoke through the prophet Isaiah and said:

"I will give them an undivided heart and put a new spirit in them; I will remove from them their heart of stone and give them a heart of flesh." (Eze 11:19 NIV.)

John Philip Newell wrote:

"[Grace] is given not to make us something other than ourselves but to make us radically ourselves. Grace is given not to implant in us a foreign wisdom but to make us alive to the wisdom that was born with us in our mother's womb. Grace is given not to lead us into another identity but to reconnect us to the beauty of our deepest identity. And grace is given not that we might find some exterior source of strength but that we might be established again in the deep inner security of our being and in learning to lose ourselves in love for one another to truly find ourselves." (8.)

That's Gospel Good News!

The evil that lurks within and without does not and will not have the final say. A Kingdom is coming; it's already here within us, where love has the run of the house. A homecoming to ourselves is in order. Our hearts are not a problem to be solved, but a treasure to be continually restored. No matter what has befallen us or what we have engaged in, healing, as miraculous as it sounds, is the truest possibility.

YOUR GOOD, GOOD HEART - PART 6
Return to Who You Really Are

Just days before he was betrayed by his people and executed by the Romans, Jesus said:

"Don't collect for yourselves treasures on earth, where moth and rust destroy and where thieves break in and steal. But collect for yourselves treasures in heaven, where neither moth nor rust destroys, and where thieves don't break in and steal. For where your treasure is, there your heart will be also." (Matt 6:19-21 HCSB.)

What is your treasure?

Jesus wasn't talking about what I was taught as a kid was a heavenly treasure chest (I even had the board game *gulp*) filled up by our good deeds that awaited us in our heavenly mansions that we would receive upon our death and acceptance into heaven (being the realm that is separate from earth). No.

The Kingdom of Heaven is not a utopia out there somewhere absent from here that God will rescue us to when we die.

For the ancient Hebrews (the men and women who wrote, and are in, the scriptures), heaven was the return to our divine and original state of shalom, peace; at one with the Divine, God, the life source, the ground of being. That's why heaven can be here and yet still coming.

"Our hearts are not a problem to be solved, but a treasure to be continually sought."

There are glimpses of it. You see it every time someone gives and loves and hopes and forgives. You see it when orphans are taken in, and widows are cared for. You see it when children are loved, and laughter is heard. You see it whenever someone listens and creates space for others to be included. You see it when mercy triumphs over judgment and when empathy crosses boundaries many dare not venture over. You see it in the sunrise, the ocean tides, the face of the moon, birds singing in the afternoon and the green grass under your feet. You see it in tragedy as people flock to help, as fridges fill with food, as shaking shoulders are held.

As dark and frightening and painful as the world is, her beauty, truth, and strength persist. Who she really is – who we really are – is still there. Deep calls unto deep, and we must remember who we were made to be.

The question is, are we going to keep valuing profits over people? Security for me over enough food and water for everyone? Are we going to continue to value image over caring for the sick and the elderly? Do we want our cities paved with gold or our homes filled with peace?

"For your heart will always pursue what you treasure" (Matt 6:21 TPT). And from your heart springs your whole life.

World change starts first and foremost with personal transformation. That stoney hard heart? Broken and corroded by sin and shame and loneliness and hurt? Jesus showed us the way to peace, healing, and wholeness. It starts with love. Love yourself through the change. Change because your life is worth more than to be used up on work that divides and breaks.

Return to who you really are, child of God.

Healed. Divine. Holy. Good.

What you believe about yourself changes everything.

YOUR GOOD, GOOD HEART - PART 7
The Origin of Goodness

Where's your heart at?

What do you value?

You might have to analyse your money habits, the words you use, how you spend your time, what and who has your attention, to get a good idea of what your true treasures are.

What do you believe about your heart?

Can you follow it? Listen to it? Attend to it, love it, heal it?

The good news is, God sees your heart. Through all the pain that you feel and that you've caused, the anger and joy, the grief and the beauty, the work and the play and the confusion and the change: God sees you. Grace seeks to remind you - she whispers in your ear, shouts it from the rooftops - of who you really are: loved.

You were created from an origin of goodness and strength and grace and peace. And to that place, you'll return your whole life long. There's no condemnation or exploitation in the seeing. God knows, and God loves, and God heals. God is present with us and to us in love. We are graciously grander than we know.

Your good, good heart is the heart of the matter. If only we all understood this, we just might be able to change the world.

"Courage, dear heart." Wrote CS Lewis (9).

There is hope.

"DO YOUR LITTLE BIT OF GOOD WHERE YOU ARE; IT'S THOSE LITTLE BITS OF GOOD PUT TOGETHER THAT OVERWHELM THE WORLD."

Desmond Tutu

"It takes courage to grow up and become who you really are." — EE Cummings

RUTH - PART 1
Once Upon a Time

Those fateful words at the start of many fairy tales, folk stories, and legends... for the ancient Hebrews, stories that began with tragedy foretold a joyous ending. The more tragic the beginning, the more joyful the outcome, and the more strange and subversive the journey between.

Once upon a time, back in the days when Israel was lead by Judges, there was a famine in the land (from Ruth 1:1 MSG).

No family was left untouched. Elimelech, Naomi, and their two sons, Mahlon and Kilion, had decided to leave Israel to find relief from their tribulations in Moab. But tragedy struck there, too. After marrying Moabite women, Mahlon, and Kilion, and their father Elimelech, died. All three of them. Dead. Their wives: Ruth, Orpah (the Moabite women), and Naomi, had some decisions to make.

The reason why they had decisions to make was that Naomi was an Israelite living in Moab. Orpah and Ruth were Moabite widows of Israelite men.

A few notes before we go further:

- Legend has it that Ruth was a Moabite princess. She had means and options.
- Elimelech and his family broke the law by leaving Israel to live in Moab. Some would have considered their actions to be selfish and heretical.
- Not only did they break the law by leaving Israel, but also by the sons marrying foreign women.
- Naomi was widowed. Yes. And I'm sure like me you've heard many sermons about how poor Naomi was destitute and faced living out her days on the streets, in slavery, or worse. But when she arrived back in Israel, we discover that she too, was a woman with means: she had family - wealthy family - who by law and tradition, had to provide for her.

This story is disruptive for many different reasons from the very beginning. Unlike the books of Nehemiah and Ezra which are exclusionary in context, Ruth, and its sister book, Isaiah, focus on inclusion. By stating at the front end of the story that Israelites were living in Moab, and had married Moabites, and that one of those Moabites had decided to return to Israel to live and worship and die as a Jew, you can assume that you're going to be taken to some confronting, beautiful, subversive, places.

Arguably, the most famous lines of this story are Ruth's in a declaration of her commitment to Naomi:

"Where you go, I go; and where you live, I'll live. Your people are my people, your God is my god; where you die, I'll die, and that's where I'll be buried, so help me God—not even death itself is going to come between us!" (Ruth 1:16-17 MSG.)

This scripture has been recited at weddings, leadership meetings, and from pulpits as a way of declaring allegiance. I've heard it preached that unless you have that kind of commitment to God, Church, and even your leader, you're not serious about your faith. I've sung this line in worship songs, chanted it at the top of my lungs: Where you go, I'll go.

But the Divine has always whispered back: I'm not going anywhere, I'm already here.

This isn't a passage about leadership. It's not a story about commitment or allegiance. This is a tale of love, and belonging, and community. Of choosing a path and walking it all the way home.

Generations earlier, Abram heard the voice of God - one that his community didn't recognise - and embarked on a journey to a place he didn't know, to a destination he wasn't sure of. Abram and Ruth bring a story of separation and division full circle. And it's much more than a leadership lesson. It's about integration, agency, and the importance of not being ruthless.

RUTH - PART 2
Where is Courage Leading You?

Ruth was a woman who made a choice.

Her first decision was marrying an Israelite. Well, Okay... maybe that was her father's choice, we don't know. But a decision was made that Ruth would marry outside of her tribe. We know the cultural implications for her husband, but what about for her? What did her family and community think? In the ancient Hebrew tradition, it's believed that Ruth was a Moabite Princess. She was wealthy, she was an aristocrat, she was used to the finer things in life. Was this a way to connect the tribes? Did Elimelech mean to provide himself a way forward for his family through their fortuitous union?

What does it usually mean in a 'heroes-journey-type-tale' when someone marries outside of the expected pool? Perhaps Ruth had more spunk and tenacity and curiosity than we have previously given her credit for.

The next decision she made was definitely her own.

After her husband died, and her husband's brother and father died too, her mother-in-law, Naomi, told Ruth to return home. The Jewish custom was that the closest male relative of the deceased husband would marry the widow. But all the nearby male relatives of Naomi's had died. There was no one left to take Ruth in. Naomi wasn't sure if she'd be welcomed home since their departure from Israel wasn't exactly culturally celebrated. Naomi believed that Ruth, and her sister-in-law, Orpah, would be better off staying in Moab and remarrying there.

There were a lot of considerations and questions for Ruth, who found herself a widow stuck between two cultures. Should she stay, or should she go?

We've all faced that decision, whether it's been in relationships, business, education, dreams or goals or family. Many people stay where they are for many different reasons. Sometimes those reasons are legitimate and lead to the right choice of continuing. Sometimes those reasons are excuses and distractions and fears and worries. Sometimes it's faith to stay, sometimes it's faith to go.

How do you know what choice to make?

In the Biblical text, the imagery of Exodus and freedom, of leaving one place to enter into a new and promised one, is a common theme. Abraham, who was part of Ruth and Naomi's heritage, as we'll discover in the coming parts, paved the way for Ruth. He embarked on a spiritual quest, not knowing where he was going, the particulars of why, or how he was going to make it.

Ruth didn't know where she was going, the particulars of why, or how she was going to make it. Israel had been in famine. It was the "time of the judges" (Ruth 1:1), and if you remember correctly, they were not easy or peaceful times.

And yet, Ruth made a decision that she was going to follow Naomi and make a life with her, come what may. Was it about conversion? Salvation?

Maybe. At its core, I think Ruth's decision was grounded in love and kindness and loyalty. Not just to the God she had met through the Jewish family she'd married into, but to the woman who had become her family. Which is how, of course, you love God best: by loving those around you. It's the genuinely courageous thing to do.

To answer the question: How do you know when to stay, or when to go? Ask yourself: where is courage leading you?

Here's the thing with strength and courage and faith: it rarely feels that way in the beginning. To start off, it feels like risk and madness and mess and wonder.

EE Cummings wrote:

"It takes courage to grow up and become who you really are."

I think courage is precisely what Ruth discovered as she looked into Naomi's eyes and said:

"Where you go, I go."

RUTH - PART 3

Have the Courage to Surrender.

After the men in her husband's family died, and her mother-in-law Naomi decided to return home to Israel, Ruth, for whatever reasons, decided to go with her. But Naomi tried to talk her and Orpah into staying in Moab. She said:

"Go back, my dear daughters. Why would you come with me? Do you suppose I still have sons in my womb who can become your future husbands? Go back, dear daughters— on your way, please! I'm too old to get a husband. Why, even if I said, 'There's still hope!' And this very night got a man and had sons, can you imagine being satisfied to wait until they were grown? Would you wait that long to get married again? No, dear daughters; this is a bitter pill for me to swallow—more bitter for me than for you. God has dealt me a hard blow." (Ruth 1:11-13 MSG.)

If this is a story about conversion and salvation, shouldn't have Naomi celebrated Ruth's decision to return with her? To commit to Judaism in knowledge and practice? To be a companion and help to her through what would be the most challenging journey of her life?

In Joseph Campbell's book, "The Hero with a Thousand Faces," he outlined the stages of 'The Hero's Journey,' as he observed them to be in most mythologies and stories from different cultures and religions around the world. He said that 'The Journey' often begins with tragedy or lack or the experience of something being taken away, creating a sense of loss and emptiness. The 'Hero' will feel a call, a yearning for adventure, something beyond what they are currently experiencing, to bridge the gap that recent events have opened up inside of them.

A crucial stage of the 'Hero's Journey' is the resistance they face to step out. After making the decision to embark on an adventure, a healing journey, to pursue what is missing, it's not like the world opens up for our heroes and grants them their desires no questions asked. No. Nobody would watch that movie. And

nobody has lived that kind of life. Usually, the first thing that happens is that all the doors slam and the all the roads close. The hero's determination to pursue their dream/desire/adventure/call come what may is essential to their success. And usually, as it happens, enduring the obstacles is where greater success than the arrival takes place: personal development and growth Ancient Hebrews (and still today) actively tried to dissuade converts, not to be exclusionary, but to ensure that the proselyte:

1) Made the choice for themselves (agency).
2) Entered into the decision with eyes wide open and a sense of engagement.
3) Were determined and committed to the transformation that was before them.

Perhaps Naomi's words to Ruth weren't selfless in the sense that Naomi was trying to make Ruth (and Orpah) stay in Moab because she believed it would be the best thing for them. But was more a test of will and determination. To see if they really meant what they said and had the tenacity to follow through.

These days, in our churches and congregations, we are so quick to accept a positive response to Jesus, we rarely take the time to work through the details. We make the numbers of hands in the air at an altar call more important than personal transformation. We think the 'Sinner's Prayer' is the gateway to salvation, rather than focusing on the continual 'Hero's Journey' of change and becoming.

Ruth is the unlikely hero of an ancient Hebrew story. A Moabite princess, a foreigner, an outsider, a widow, and a woman. She embarks on a hero's journey, where progress is the continued commitment to overcoming, not just obstacles from without, but the temptation within to take the (short-term) easy way out. But rather than her story being about finding heroes in unlikely places, it challenges our propensity to judge some people as "unlikely" heroes.

A hero isn't someone who looks a certain way or has a certain IQ, or comes from a particular place and can do specific things. *"We must be willing to get rid of the life we've planned, so as to have the life that is waiting for us. The old skin has to be shed before the new one can come."* Said Joseph Campbell (1).

In other words, a hero is anyone who has the courage to surrender.

RUTH - PART 4
A Subversive and Radical Idea

In his book "The Hero with a Thousand Faces," Joseph Campbell outlined the rolling plot and theme to all the great myths, stories, and adventures told throughout history, culture, and religion, the world over. They all seem to follow a particular pattern. It seems to be a transcendent sequence that plays out in our lives, too, if we choose to embark on the journey.

The four stages of the Hero's Journey, according to Joseph Campbell, are:

1). Separation: the experience of lack or loss or emptiness.
2). The descent into the abyss: crossing the threshold from decision to practice that generally takes us to places of confrontation and difficulty.
3). The ascent: where flow starts to happen, the second wind of strength.
4). Unification: the return or the resurrection. The culmination of events into a transcendent outcome.

I highlight all that to say this: Historically and traditionally, most 'hero journey' stories feature men, or the masculine, as the protagonist. Women play a role but rarely do they function as the central character.

But not in the Bible.

The Bible is a strange library of books. On the one hand, some passages and stories seem so backward and exclusionary, and then beside those, you have these radically progressive books of inclusion and beauty and transcendence. Ruth is one such book and story. It challenges our perceptions and the origin of them. Even Joseph Campbell admitted that women were rarely "heroes." They just had too much to do, he said, to be able to fathom adventure.

BUT, we have Ruth.

Many believe that the story of Ruth is about the adherence and commitment to Torah (the law). Ruth, a foreigner, an outsider, committed herself to God, and the Jewish way of life, highlighting the magnitude and import of our commitment to keeping the law. If a foreigner so strongly bound herself to it, how much more should those born and bred of the tribe?

But this explanation leaves a few things wanting: Firstly, it's dualistic in its vision of the foreigner and the Jew. And it's not a story about adherence to Torah only. This is not a story of comparison but integration. Ruth bound herself to a living, breathing, flesh, and blood, human, not a list of do's and don'ts. She made a commitment to Naomi.

Electricity and sound waves had already been discovered by the time Thomas Edison and Graham Bell got involved. Yet without those two geniuses, the knowledge of electricity and sound waves would not have been integrated into the world we live in. In the Hebrew tradition, there is a unique genius involved in the exploitation and proliferation of ideas, just as there is a genius in their discovery. This is known as 'Binah,' often translated as "understanding," and in ancient tradition, it is the unique property of women.

Rashi (a famous and influential Rabbi and Jewish commentator of the Talmud) explained that Jewish women are the Jewish house. The ideas of Judaism come to life in the Jewish home and are translated into reality by the guidance of Jewish women. It's where knowledge becomes practice.

It's about balance and integration. Knowledge and practice go hand in hand. You can have the law, and say that you're committed to it, but to actually understand it in your living, as you live, is a different thing entirely. And clearly, when you're living it, some rules are fit to break. Hello, Ruth.

This is what Ruth represents: the integration of knowledge and practice. She bound herself to Judaism by linking herself to Naomi (broke a few Torah laws by doing so) in fact, you can't have one without the other. Spirit and matter can't be separated. The challenge is to not just talk about embarking on a hero's journey; discussing the importance of 'this' and 'that,' but of actually picking up our lives, putting skin in the game, and doing the work.

Which is just as a subversive and radical of an idea now

"I think true success is intrinsic... It's love. It's kindness. It's community." —Tom Shadyac

RUTH - PART 5
Lead with Kindness

Ruth left Moab after her husband, brother-in-law, and father-in-law, died. She walked side by side with her Israelite mother-in-law, Naomi, through the hills and desert to a land she didn't know and wasn't sure she'd be accepted in. She made a choice, she took a risk, and she put her life behind it.

When they arrived in Israel, they were met unexpectedly well. Ruth told Naomi that she would go out and find food in the fields that were being harvested, and she ended up serendipitously in the fields of Boaz, whom she didn't know was a relative of Naomi's, whose own wife had passed away, and was in a position to marry her.

In ancient Judaism, there were various regulations around harvest time about leaving leftovers in the fields so that the "the widow, the poor, and the stranger" would be able to come after the harvesters, pick up the leftovers, and have something to eat. On the day that Ruth found Boaz's field, she also found herself the recipient of these regulations, and the story goes that she went home with an ephah of grain. An ephah of grain is about 15kg or 33lb, which in ancient Hebrew literature, is a nod to generosity, and overflowing kindness.

More than anything, Ruth's interactions with Boaz that day were a picture of "chessed," the Hebrew word for 'loving kindness.' She had shown great kindness to Naomi by committing herself to her and the life they would create. They became sisters, in a way.

I like to picture them walking home to Israel arms and hearts linked, afraid and unsure but moving forward anyway, finding courage and tenacity in each other's presence. What Ruth received from Boaz was that same kind of 'chessed.' The fact that she was a woman, a widow, and a stranger, didn't matter. Kindness should have no regulations, no boundaries. Kindness makes heroes of everyone.

From there, Ruth and Boaz's relationship progressed. Boaz was about forty years older than Ruth. He was wealthy, he was a relative; he had the means and position to take Ruth, and her mother in law, in and build a life together.

What happened next comes under a lot of scrutiny. Under Naomi's instruction, Ruth went to the threshing floor (the barn) at night, where Boaz and his employees were sleeping, and 'presented' herself to him.

She was to wait until everyone was asleep, go to the feet of Boaz, uncover them, and wait to see what he would do. There are two camps of thought here. One is that the uncovering of feet was an act of surrender and humility: Ruth was making herself humbly available to Boaz. The second idea is that uncovering feet was a euphemism in ancient Judaism for a sexual act or advance. And that Ruth literally created physical vulnerability and intimacy between them, which put Boaz in the position to need to marry her. People go on and on about which one it is. At the end of the day, I think we spend too much time worrying about the sexual details of people's lives, and not enough about the vulnerability, the love, and the kindness with which we treat each other. Perhaps the details here are ambiguous for a reason.

It comes down to this:

Ruth was an agent of kindness and 'faith in practice' to Naomi. Boaz was the same for Ruth. Not because he had to, or because he was the masculine hero out to save the damsel in distress, but because he was available and willing.

Practicing faith isn't about adhering to a dot point list of rules and regulations. It's about living the essence of the atmosphere those rules and regulations were designed to create, but will always fall short of explaining. You'll find more energy and life and creation and spirit in the act of kindness, then you will in hearing a speech about it. And sometimes it's in breaking the rules that the essence of the rule shines through all the more.

Boaz didn't save Ruth. They are together a picture of integration and flow; a mural of the world you create when you live and lead with kindness that trumps propriety.

"Do your little bit of good where you are; it's those little bits of good put together that overwhelm the world."

Said Bishop Desmond Tutu.

"If you want to be holy, be kind."
—*Frederick Buechner*

RUTH - PART 6
Even When It's Broken

Every May on the Jewish calendar is the festival of Shavuot, which is around the same time we (all faiths that claim Christian status) observe Pentecost. It's the celebration of the giving of Torah at Mount Sinai. And do you know what passage of scripture they read at the festival every year as the primary text?

Ruth.

Her story represents the integration of law and practice. She embodies what is to BE, not just to KNOW. She left her old life behind in pursuit of another. She made a choice, she embarked on a journey, and she transformed. She committed herself to Naomi, and in doing so, she committed not just her intellect, but her life and practice to Judaism, too.

Any faith - all spirituality - means nothing if it doesn't transform your 'practice.' You can know all the right things, memorise scripture, and even obey the law to a 'T,' like the rich young ruler who approached Jesus and asked:

"I obey all the commandments, what more should I do?"

And Jesus "fixed his gaze upon the man, with tender love, and said to him, *"Yet there is still one thing in you lacking. Go, sell all that you have and give the money to the poor. Then all of your treasure will be in heaven. After you've done this, come back and walk with me."* (Mark 10:21 TPT.)

This isn't another thing to check off on the how-to-be-a-good-Christian-list. This is about practice and surrender and what kind of life you are choosing to participate in.

One of the most significant challenges spirituality faces today is that it's becoming about the headlines and not the details. It's becoming about the dogmas and doctrines, and not about the flow of life and love.

Doctrine is the scaffold, which ebbs and flows with the rising of consciousness and the changing times; we are the building, the bricks, the materials that make the universe hum. We are a team, not a hierarchy.

Jesus idea was revolutionary, but it wasn't supposed to be. It was a return to the truth that Spirit had been witnessing to all along through the flesh and blood lives of those who made themselves available to listen.

Ruth is read at Shavuot, the festival to celebrate the law given to Moses by God, because she (as did Naomi and Boaz) showed us where the law is meant to take us... even when it's broken. Especially when it's broken.

Society cannot be made by laws alone. It needs something more — the unforced, unlegislated kindness that makes us reach out to each other, even if we are lonely and vulnerable ourselves. Then and now, society needs the kindness of strangers.

Knowledge and practice. Integration. Spirit and matter. It's never just one thing. It's a community of these. And we know we're headed in the right direction when it leads us to generosity and expansion. When we have to dig deep and get good and brave and share our lives with others. It's always a risk, it's a constant practice, it's continually a healing work in progress.

RUTH - PART 7
Willing to Cross

Every hero's journey begins with tragedy, or loss, or emptiness. The sense of something missing and the ache to fill the void. Long before Ruth was born a Moabite princess, two men that were meant to build a new life and tribe together, parted ways: Abraham and Lot. Long-and-complicated-story-short, things went south for Lot, and he ended up fathering children with his daughters. One of whom fathered the nation of Moab.

Over the years, Israel and Moab became bitter enemies. What started off as family with the intent to create something new and beautiful in the world, turned into separateness, violence, and hatred.

Naomi and Boaz were descendants of Abraham. Ruth, a descendant of Lot.

The meta-theme of the story of Ruth and Naomi and Boaz, is re-connection. Redemption. When Ruth returns to Israel, this little story birthed in tragedy becomes a story about the reunion of Lot and Abraham. Ruth coming home and marrying Boaz is about Lot coming home.

And we know this because the end of the book places particular emphasis on genealogy. We learn that Ruth and Boaz had a son they called Obed, whose wife gave birth to a son they called Jesse, whose wife gave birth to a son they named...

David.

In fact, when you look through the genealogy of Abraham, to David, to Christ, it is full of unexpected hero's that by law and propriety, should not have been there.

More than it being the idea that heroes can come from unlikely places, it's a challenge as to why we believe some to be unlikely heroes: we shouldn't expect heroes to be a specific gender, creed, code, personality, physicality, colour, or tribe. We should see each individual as they are, in all their vulnerable and glorious beauty and divinity.

This story is about how when we treat others with kindness and courage, we can't help but redeem the hero inside each of us.

There should be no place we can't expect greatness from. Not out of unrealistic expectations, but because we should believe that everyone has greatness inside of them. Redemption is always the end game. When the law gets in the way, the law should be broken.

There is a form of greatness, suggests the story and genealogy of Ruth, that has nothing to do with power, fame, or renown. It exists in simple deeds of kindness and friendship, generosity and grace. Rarely do they make the news. But they change lives, redeeming some of the pain of the human condition, and reconnecting with us with who we were always meant to be.

Ruth's name has no direct translation in Hebrew. But over the years, it has become synonymous to the

practice of loving-kindness (chessed in Hebrew) to the point where the middle English word 'ruthless' was created to mean the absence of it. If there is anything we could take away from the book of Ruth as a practice, it would be to embark on the hero's journey of "ruth-full-ness."

Be kind to yourself.
Be kind to your neighbour.
Be kind to your enemy.
Be kind to strangers.

You just might *change* the world.

REFERENCES

THE PRACTICE
1). Henry Ward Beecher, Life Thoughts (1858). p. 37.
2). Peter Enns. The Bible Tells Me So: Why Defending Scripture Has Made Us Unable to Read It (pp. 23-24). HarperOne, 2015.
3). Richard Rohr. The Naked Now. Learning to See as the Mystics See, Pg 74. Crossroad publications, 2009.
4). Desmond Tutu. No Future Without Forgiveness, Pg 230. Image, 2000.
5). 1979 February 10, New York Times, Books of The Times: Nature Has Spoken to Me by Anatole Broyard, (Book Review of "The Complete Letters of Vincent Van Gogh" in 3 Volumes), Quote Page 17, Column 3, New York.

THE OTHER SIDE
1). Rene Girard, I See Satan Fall Like Lightening. Pg 42. Orbis Books, 2001.
2). Richard Rohr. Daily Meditations can.org The Inner Witness, 10th October 2016.
3). Gerd Theissen, The Gospels in Context: Social and Political History in the Synoptic Tradition (trans. L. M. Maloney; London: T&T Clark, 2004), 110.
4). Susan Pease Banitt. The Trauma Tool Kit: Healing PTSD from the Inside Out. Pg xix. Quest Books, 2012
5). Frederick Buechner. Secrets in the Dark: A Life in Sermons, Pg 151. Harper Collins, 2007.
6). Brené Brown. The Power of Vulnerability. Teachings of Authenticity, Connection, and Courage. Audio Book. Sounds True, 2013.
7). Alexander John Shaia. Heart and Mind: The Four-Gospel Journey for Radical Transformation (p. 126). Mosaic Press, Kindle Edition, 2014.

HERE I AM
1). JK Rowling. Very Good Lives: The Fringe Benefits of Failure and the Importance of Imagination, Pg 33. Little, Brown and Company, 2015.

BEYOND THE LABEL
1). Stephen M Wylen. The Seventy Faces of Torah. Paulest Press. 2005
2). H. Stephen Shoemaker. God Stories: New Narratives from Sacred Texts. Judson Pr. 1998
3. Rob Bell. What is the Bible? How an Ancient Library of Poems, Letter, and Stories Can Transform the Way You Think and Feel About Everything. Harper Collins. Kindle edition. 2017.
4). Paul Evodkimov. The Sacrament of Love. St Vladimirs Seminary Pr. 2011.
5). Amy Jill Levine. :Short Stories by Jesus: The Enigmatic Parables of a Controversial Rabbi. Pg 239. Harper One. 2015.
6). Amy Jill Levine. Short Stories by Jesus: The Enigmatic Parables of a Controversial Rabbi. Pg Pg 221 – 246. Harper One. 2015.
7). Amy Jill Levine. :Short Stories by Jesus: The Enigmatic Parables of a Controversial Rabbi. Harper One. 2015.
8). Joshua Fields Millburn and Ryan Nicodemus, AKA: @theminimalists https://www.theminimalists.com/labels/ accessed August 2018.

YOUR GOOD, GOOD HEART
1). John Philip Newell. Christ of the Celts; The Healing of Creation. Pg 13. Wild Goose Publications. 2008.
2). Science of the Heart. Intuition Research. www.heartmath.org/research/science-of-the-heart/intuition-research/. Accessed August 2018.
3). John Philip Newell. Christ of the Celts; The Healing of Creation. Pg 9. Wild Goose Publications. 2008.
4). Martin Luther King Jnr. Strength to Love. Pg 45. Fortress Press. 2010.
5). Martin Luther King Jnr. Strength to Love. Pg 47. Fortress Press. 2010.
6). Cynthia Bourgeault. The Wisdom Jesus: Transforming Heart and Mind—A New Perspective on Christ and His Message. Pg 45. Shambhala. 2008.
7.) The Radical King by Dr. Martin Luther King, Jr. Edited and Introduced by Dr. Cornel West. Pg 57. Beacon Press. 2016.
8). John Philip Newell. Christ of the Celts; The Healing of Creation. Pg 10. Wild Goose Publications. 2008.
9). CS Lewis. The Voyage of the Dawn Treader. Pg 187. Harper Collins. 1994.

RUTH
1). Joseph Campbell. Reflections on the Art of Living: A Joseph Campbell Companion. Selected and Edited by Diane Osbon. Harper Perennial, 1995.

CREDITS

All these beautiful images come from wonderfully generous work of the incredible photographers and artists on unsplash.com - A big thank you to each of you. We couldn't have done it without you!

In order of appearance

Cover: Alex Perez
Inside Cover: Joshua Fuller
Jesse and Liz Portrait: Nate Haslem

THE PRACTICE
Clarisse Meyer, Mourizer Awad, Jen P, Hasan Almasi, Max Ostrozhinskiy, Martin Widenka, Osman Rosana

THE OTHER SIDE
Ian Froome, Daniil Silantev, Guillaume de Germain, Allan Nygren, Kyle Peyton, Riccardo Mion, Toa Heftiba, Brynden, Jeremy Allouche, Matthew Smith, Nathan Dumlao, Andreas Dress, Casey Horner

SACRIFICE AND SONS
Federica Galli, Atilla Taskiran, Rocknwool, Sarah Dorweiler, Liana Mikah, Dillon Mangum, Mike Marquez, Green Chameleon, Math, Paul Hanaoka

HERE I AM
Nathan Dumlao, Jon Tyson, Brandon Wong, Nathan Dumlao, Nathan Dumlao, Kunj Parekh, Chanan Greenblatt, Marc Steenbeke

BEYOND THE LABEL
Tracey Hocking, Jean Philippe Delberghe, Imani Clovis, Han Chenxu, Max Di Capua, Monika Grabkowska, Henry Co, JJ Ying, Raoul Croes, Nordwood Themes, Sylvie Tittel

WHAT'S NEXT
Ishan Seefromthesky, Alex Perez, Sacha Styles, Eberhard Grossgasteiger, Mathyas Kurmann, Angelo Pantazis, Ishan Seefromthesky

YOUR GOOD, GOOD HEART
Chris Lee, Adrienne Leonard, Ap X 90, Sylvie Tittel, Sarah Dorweiler, Scott Webb, Corinne Kutz, Lauren Mancke

RUTH
John Jason, Joris Berthelot, Resa Cahya, Jacalyn Beales, Max Ostrozhinskiy, Natanja Grun, Pierre Chatel Innocenti, John Jason

Thank You page: Jack B

THANKYOU

Six years ago we started posting devotions and designs on Instagram thinking that our family and friends would patronise us enough to like them. All these years later it has grown into a beautiful community of people seeking more of their spirituality than platitudes, cliché's and catch phrases. Without you; without our readers and supporters and App subscribers and social media friends/followers and emailers and website commenters... well, you guys have taught us so much, and given us so much encouragement and life and strength; our deepest gratitude and thanks goes to you. Thank you for making this journey possible, and for making it beautiful and meaningful.

This humble little book represents the work and influence of many. So much thanks to my husband and partner in all the things, Jesse, who directed this project and put so many hours into creating it. And for equal parts loving me and pushing me to get the work done. I love you. To my friends who keep me honest and laugh at my jokes and put up with my crazy angsty text messaging... you're never getting rid of me. I love you. Huge thanks to my badass friend Jessica Smith for continually encouraging me and helping me edit this baby of mine. To be able to trust someone with your words is no small thing. My kids won't ever read this, but big thanks to them, too. They've taught me nearly everything I know. And they're spunky as anything. You would love them.

Liz
xx

www.ingramcontent.com/pod-product-compliance
Lightning Source LLC
Chambersburg PA
CBHW042033030526
44107CB00094B/2994